I know of no individual who is being more used by the Holy Spirit to reach across the whole of the Middle East world with the dynamic hope wrapped in the message of the gospel.

—JACK HAYFORD
FOUNDING PASTOR, THE CHURCH ON THE WAY
CHANCELLOR, THE KING'S COLLEGE AND SEMINARY
LOS ANGELES, CALIFORNIA

I have traveled with Elias from Ur to Jerusalem, Damascus to London. He is an amazing man . . . with a mission. The life, travel, and passion of Elias Malki to evangelize a chosen part of the world remind me of a twenty-first century apostle Paul.

—CLAUD BOWERS
SUPERCHANNEL TELEVISION
ORLANDO, FLORIDA

Dr. Malki has a riveting story to tell! It's about the specialness of all people . . . especially those in the turbulent and often misunderstood world of the Middle East. I've seen the magnificent results firsthand and encourage everyone to read of God's life-transforming love and power.

—JIM TOLLE
SENIOR PASTOR, THE CHURCH ON THE WAY
VAN NUYS, CALIFORNIA

BRINGING GOOD NEWS TO THE MIDDLE EAST

AMBASSADOR
OF A
HIGHER
POWER

BRINGING GOOD NEWS TO THE MIDDLE EAST

AMBASSADOR
OF A
HIGHER POWER

ELIAS MALKI

Charisma
HOUSE
A STRANG COMPANY

Most Strang Communications/Charisma House/Siloam products are available at special quantity discounts for bulk purchase for sales promotions, premiums, fund-raising, and educational needs. For details, write Strang Communications/ Charisma House/Siloam, 600 Rinehart Road, Lake Mary, Florida 32746, or telephone (407) 333-0600.

Ambassador of a Higher Power by Elias Malki
Published by Charisma House
A Strang Company
600 Rinehart Road
Lake Mary, Florida 32746
www.charismahouse.com

Unless otherwise noted, all Scripture quotations are from the King James Version of the Bible.

Scripture quotations marked AMP are from the Amplified Bible. Old Testament copyright © 1965, 1987 by the Zondervan Corporation. The Amplified New Testament copyright © 1954, 1958, 1987 by the Lockman Foundation. Used by permission.

Cover design by Rachel Campbell

Library of Congress Cataloging-in-Publication Data
Malki, Elias.
  Ambassador of a higher power / Elias Malki.
      p. cm.
  ISBN 1-59185-798-8 (pbk.)
  1. Malki, Elias. 2. Missionaries--Middle East--Biography. I.
Title.
  BV3152.5.M35A3 2005
  266'.0092--dc22

                                    2005012558

06 07 08 09 — 9 8 7 6 5 4 3 2 1
Printed in the United States of America

DEDICATION

I dedicate this book to my Lord and Savior, Jesus Christ, who has enabled me, counted me faithful, and put me into the ministry (1 Timothy 1:12), and to my wife, Donna, and four children, Rebecca, Ruth, Timothy, and Daniel, who helped me in the ministry through the years. Also to the many friends who encouraged me to write this book and those who helped with typing and proofreading. And to every person who reads this book, my prayer is that you will remember that what God did for me He will do for you—because one person with God is a majority.

Now then we are ambassadors for Christ, as though God did beseech you by us: we pray you in Christ's stead, be ye reconciled to God.

—2 CORINTHIANS 5:20

For which I am an ambassador in bonds: that therein I may speak boldly, as I ought to speak.

—EPHESIANS 6:20

CONTENTS

FOREWORD

As high a commendation as the New Testament ever gives a leader is found in the words the ancient Council of Jerusalem spoke concerning Barnabas and Paul. When determining how they might best urge those to whom they came to listen and heed these two apostles, the rest of the apostolic band affirmed them by saying they were "men who have hazarded their lives for the sake of our Lord Jesus Christ" (Acts 15:26, AMP).

You are holding a book in your hands that has been written by a man who meets that same standard. Elias Malki deserves a hearing by any thoughtful person in this twenty-first century just as certainly as Paul and Barnabas did in the first century. His fidelity to the Word of God and the testimony of

Jesus, constantly upheld and declared in the Middle East for a full half-century, classifies him as a contemporary church leader worthy of high regard, support, and a serious hearing.

"THE WORLD HAS YET TO SEE
WHAT GOD CAN DO THROUGH ONE
MAN WHO DOESN'T CARE WHO
GETS THE CREDIT."

I have known Elias and his wife, Donna, since our days together as students in Los Angeles when he and I were studying for the ministry. His devotion to advancing the gospel in the Middle East, at a time when it was not nearly as focused as it is today on the whole church's bulletin board, was born of unshakeable conviction. That sense of mission compelled its labors for years—years when, "in a dry and thirsty land where no water is," he was seldom rewarded with a positive response. But notwithstanding the long and arduous task of plowing the fields to open the way to the gospel's spread, and beyond the seasons of suffering and rejection he experienced, Elias labored on. He never reneged from the certainty of his call and never winced when called to stand faithful for his Savior, always looking forward to a day of divine grace and visitation.

Pursuant upon and beyond the earlier, more difficult times, the past fifteen years have seen a growing penetration of his ministry through his television, radio, and church leadership training ministries. Middle East Gospel

Outreach, the formal name of Elias Malki's ministry, is a study in how effectively God can cause the simplicity of "the truth as it is in Jesus" to impact lives in miracle power and soul-transforming glory. I know of no individual who is being more used by the Holy Spirit to reach across the whole of the Arab world with the dynamic hope wrapped in the message of the gospel.

In a day when dramatic development of buildings, programs, and personalities tend to dominate the thoughts of so many who observe the church in our time, I lament the frequency with which the true heroes of our era are overlooked. God sees them, however, and I believe He is calling us all back—back to the same simplicity that resonates to the heart of God and proliferates the spread of the message of His Son into the tough-to-reach, high-risk arenas of ministry.

As you read, I believe your heart will be touched. The record of God's grace through Elias is not a boastful report, but simply a reminder of D. L. Moody's words: "The world has yet to see what God can do through one man who doesn't care who gets the credit." Here is just one example of God at work in such a man, and knowing Elias as I do, he invites you to read these pages only for your encouragement.

I believe you will be built up in faith, summoned to service, and focused in vision to reach your place of ministry for Jesus' sake. And I also believe that as you read of his experiences and labors, your heart will be touched, and when it is, I guarantee you: Elias won't ask for the credit!

—JACK W. HAYFORD
FOUNDING PASTOR, THE CHURCH ON THE WAY
CHANCELLOR, THE KING'S COLLEGE AND SEMINARY
LOS ANGELES, CALIFORNIA

Chapter 1

THE BLOOD OF THE MARTYRS

THE NIGHT BEFORE the murderous mob arrived in his village, my father, Aziz, narrowly escaped by horseback, fleeing with the other Christian men to a safe haven where, they prayed, the Kurdish warriors bent on jihad would not find them.

It was just before the end of World War I, and the Turkish sultan had called for holy war against Christians because of suspicions that Christians who held positions in the Turkish government were a danger to the security of the Muslim nation. Many Muslims turned against their Christian neighbors, and makeshift armies of radical warriors scoured the country, looking for Christians and giving them a stark choice: reject Jesus and accept Muhammad, or be killed on the spot. The Christians, including those in my family, had no recourse but to flee—and if they were caught, they could only hope the mobs would spare their lives. My father and uncles fled, but my grandfather, John Malki, stayed behind, perhaps to care for the widows and children, or perhaps because he did not believe the jihad would be carried out in Karadesh.

It was a choice that would put his life on the line.

John was an Assyrian, whose country of ancestry, Assyria, is now known as northern Iraq. He accepted Jesus Christ as his Savior through a Presbyterian missionary in eastern Turkey, then devoted himself to the gospel and became the first missionary to the small coastal village of Karadesh, Turkey. The people there loved him because of his compassion and because he had established a school for their children. Though the town was overwhelmingly Muslim, John had lived there in peace and was pastor of a small Presbyterian church. His wife had died some years earlier.

But the holy warriors did arrive, and they were incensed to find the Christian men gone.

"Cowards!" they said, stomping around the village. "They do not really believe in their God, or they would have stayed and fought. As it is, they left the women and children here."

As the day wore on and the house searches proved less and less fruitful, the warriors changed tactics. They appeared to calm down. John, whose life was in mortal danger, observed them warily as they gathered to talk. The villagers watched, worn out from the volatility that had permeated the small town since word of the jihad had arrived. They had begged

John earlier to convert to Islam so his life would be spared, but John would not consider it.

"No," he had said, waving off the mere suggestion of it. "I am Christ's, and He is mine. That is all."

Then one of the warriors approached him, wearing a smile.

"We have changed our minds," he said. "We are tired of this bloodshed. Send word to the young men that they may come back, and then we will make peace and leave. This is not true jihad."

"I AM CHRIST'S, AND HE IS MINE. THAT IS ALL."

John knew better than to take their word, but more men gathered around. He felt their heat, smelled their sweat. They had spent their energy for now. Their arms were slack, the swords no longer flashing about as when they had first arrived. The spirit of war seemed to have departed. Perhaps it was a sign of hope.

"OK," John said, knowing it was probably useless to resist, even if he had tried. To speak contrary to their wishes might reignite their anger; as it was, he had a chance to make peace. "I will send word."

He sent a messenger to the safe haven to tell the men to return. My uncle Simeon had fled with his family by a different route and was already gone. Aziz and his brother Solomon quarreled when they heard the message promising peace.

"You have to be kidding," said Aziz. "These men are luring us down to kill us."

"But what if everything is returning to normal?" Solomon said. "At least they are not pretending to leave, then ambushing us when we return. They want to see us face-to-face. It is harder to kill a man when you have looked into his eyes."

But Aziz was unconvinced. Solomon prepared his horse, then looked at his brother one more time.

"Are you coming with us?" he said, referring to the other men saddled up around him.

"No," said Aziz. "I don't trust the warriors."

"Even though our father says all is well?"

Aziz shook his head slowly.

"I am leaving this country," he said. "I am tired of violence and the threats of violence. This is an uneasy, dangerous place to spend one's life."

They embraced, and the riders galloped downhill. My father turned the other way and planned his route through the mountains to the sea. He would take a ship somewhere—anywhere—to escape the wave of blood that had overwhelmed his beloved country.

It did not take long for the Christian men who had returned to realize they had been tricked. The Kurdish Muslims seized Solomon almost without hesitation and ran him through with a sword. Then they gave John a final opportunity to deny his Lord. He was forced to his knees in the dust of the street, and a Kurdish Muslim held a sword to his neck.

"You have a choice. You may live or die," the man said. "If you wish to live, accept Islam."

Onlookers from John's church and Sunday school watched in fear from windows and doorways, though they dared not weep. As sunlight glinted off the razor-sharp blade, there was no one left to plead for his life.

With the blade poised at his neck, John did not hesitate to reply:

"I will live and die for Christ. I will not deny my Savior."

MORE THAN ONE AND A HALF MILLION TURKISH CHRISTIANS LOST THEIR LIVES IN THAT HOLY WAR, CALLED THE *ARMENIAN MASSACRE.*

Those were his last words. Immediately, the warrior brought the sword swiftly back and forth, cutting off John's head. His body slumped to the ground. Among those watching was a thirteen-year-old girl who had attended John's Sunday school. One of the terrorists had taken her and made her a wife to one of his sons. She buried her face in her arm, unable to witness any more of the scene's horror.

It was only the beginning of bloodshed. All the Christians who had stayed in Karadesh and those who returned there from the safe haven were killed. More than one and a half million Turkish Christians lost their lives in that holy war, called the *Armenian Massacre* because more Armenian Christians died than any other nationality.

The blood that ran in the dust of Karadesh that day was

martyrs' blood. My grandfather and uncle were dead. My father escaped to Beirut, Lebanon, which is where I was born. I grew up knowing only scant details of my grandfather's death, but it was enough to send chills up my back whenever I pictured him preaching the gospel almost single-handedly in that tiny Turkish outpost. Of all the heroes and tales of conquest I heard about as a child, none stood higher in my imagination than my grandfather. Perhaps his story should have warned me away from the perilous work of spreading the gospel in the Middle East. But rather than shrink from the danger, when the time came, I took up the same burden he had borne and followed his path as a missionary to the Middle East. I too would experience near-death escapes, heartbreak, and triumph as I partnered with God to bring the good news to one of the most hostile regions in the world.

When I was born my family lived in Lebanon, right next door to a palm reader. She was one of the superstitious people in our neighborhood who whispered that I had come at precisely the wrong time for my family. The Great Depression had settled on the world like a thick cloak, robbing people of money, health, and dreams. My father—a construction contractor, a lay preacher in the Presbyterian church, and an uncompromising man of fearsome physical strength—was among those working his body to exhaustion to scratch out a living for his expanding family. At the time of my birth, finding work in Lebanon was hard enough without the concern of feeding another child. Now the celebration of my entrance into the world was tinged with anxiety: How would he and my mother feed us all?

Would I even survive to adulthood? When would the curse of the Depression end?

Money was so scarce in our household that my mother had begun working in the fields when I was still in the womb. Under normal circumstances, my father would have been far too proud to allow her to gather crops by hand, bending over for hours under the merciless Middle Eastern sun. In a country where women rarely labored as men did, it would have brought shame on my family. But he felt he had no choice, and so he allowed her to join the harvesters picking grapes, figs, and stalks of grain while I grew inside of her. As her pregnancy began to show, her movements became more awkward and conspicuous, and he could sense our family's reputation sinking by degrees as our desperation became obvious. But because the hardship was so widespread in those days, cultural customs often bowed to economic reality. Unusual steps became necessary, not just for us, but for all people in Lebanon, and so most people were kind enough to look the other way—a common grace that soothed the raw tempers and frayed nerves that prevailed in our home and, as best as we could tell, in the entire world beyond.

When I was born, I was weak and sickly from the start. Mom, who possessed a keen business sense, continued to work hard after I was born, and as she strained to keep the family fed, I sometimes languished from lack of attention. Dad took the drastic step of going to Palestine to look for work. When I was six months old, he came home one day, defeated and nearly asleep on his feet with fatigue, and found Mom holding me. There was a strange rattling in my throat.

"He is not well," she said.

"What is it?" he asked, steeling himself for yet another blow.

She brought me to her shoulder and rubbed my back. I was too feverish to cry.

"I think it's pneumonia," she said. And it was—a life-threatening case.

> ## BUT MY MOTHER HAD HAD ENOUGH.... SHE TOOK ME IN HER ARMS AND SAID FIRMLY, "NO, MY SON WILL LIVE."

When our neighbor the palm reader heard that I was gravely ill, she came over straightaway, like a fly drawn to rotting fruit. She smartly took me in her hands, looked over my frail frame, and listened to the sickness in my lungs. Then she smiled, acquitting herself like an expert. She was proud of her self-appointed position as neighborhood seer.

"This baby should die," she pronounced with satisfaction.

They both looked at me, as if I would provide the "yea" or "nay" to her judgment. I was hardly there at all. My skin burned with the illness. Every part of me, from my neck to my ankles, was so thin—much thinner than my three older brothers had been.

"If you are smart," the neighbor continued, "you won't

take him to that doctor in Beirut tomorrow like you plan to."

My mother considered her words. Mom had been raised completely differently than my father, whose black-and-white Christian beliefs guided every decision he made. She was the daughter of a mortgage company owner, and she knew the art of business and compromise, of being practical, of knowing when to let a deal go. She had been raised Greek Orthodox and did not yet know Jesus personally. Rather, she knew finances, money, how to make things work in a pinch.

As she thought about the neighbor's words, they made hard, economic sense: I had never been healthy. Perhaps I never would be. I might be one of those babies who burden down a family. Who knew how long the economic hardship would last? What if the rest of my family suffered because of me? And what if I ended up dying anyway?

But Mom was also intuitive and compassionate, and her hunch told her something was not right. Behind the palm reader's eyes lurked some evil logic; the woman's insincere smile alarmed her. The two women stood there looking at me in silence. The streets outside seemed eerily quiet. In the invisible realm between them, two visions of my future vied for control.

"Let him die," the neighbor said again. "Otherwise, he is only going to cause you a lot of trouble."

It was as if she had thrust a dagger into my mother's weakest argument. But my mother had had enough. She seized on her gut reaction, and a stubbornness rose up within her. She took me in her arms and said firmly, "No, my son will live."

The neighbor, surprised by my mother's sudden force-fulness, muttered her dissatisfaction and left our home. If I lived, she would tell nobody what she had said to my mother—she couldn't afford the loss of reputation. But if I died, she would make sure the whole neighborhood knew about the encounter and that her pronouncement had been correct.

That night the palm reader's words haunted our house-hold as I became hotter and sicker than I had ever been. My father, red-eyed and wordless, tried to help clear my lungs, but as he and Mom attended to me, it was plain to both of them that I had little chance of living through the night. The closest doctor was in Beirut, an hour away. They had to wait until morning.

Before dawn, my mother took me by public transporta-tion to the doctor. When she finally arrived, through dusty Arab streets on a bus crowded with people hoping to find work in the city, the doctor took me in his hands, and an expression of astonishment and relief crossed his face.

"If you had waited any longer to bring this baby in, he would have died," he said. "It's a good thing you came when you did."

He began to check me more thoroughly and to write out a prescription. My tired mother could only think back to the previous day's conversation with our neighbor. It seemed so clear to her now that something had tried to insinuate itself in our home and take my life; the neighbor's sinister advice had arrived at the precise moment of my greatest vulnerability.

When the doctor had finished, Mom returned home with me in her arms and with a prescription for a home remedy.

It worked. By the next morning, the fever had disappeared, and I was healthy again. The neighbor did not speak of it, but my father told anyone who would listen that God had spared the life of his youngest son.

~ↄ Chapter 2 ↄ~

REBELLION...AND REPENTANCE

W HEN I WAS three years old, the Depression drove
my family to Palestine, and we crossed the border of Lebanon on camels to meet my father who
had established a home for us in the beautiful seaport city
of Haifa. We lived in a cinder block house by the sea, with
olive trees and paved roads and the delightful smell of the
ocean permeating the air. Then we moved to the country
where the roads were only dirt, but our house was much
bigger. In each home, we slept in one room and stacked our
cotton mattresses up during the day. There was no such
thing as privacy, and soon our family would include eleven
children. We enjoyed one another and had the blessing of
the Lord, in spite of financial hardships.

My father took us to church and Sunday school every Sunday, and when the Presbyterians didn't have church on Sunday night he took us to other evangelical churches—the Nazarene, Christian Missionary Alliance, and Brethren meetings. I knew from the start that we were different from the people around us. The British occupied Palestine at that time, and there were very few Jews. Most people there were Arabs, mostly Muslims, with a fair number of Greek Orthodox Christians, Catholics, and a smattering of Protestants. But in my family, unlike most, Sunday was our Sabbath day, and, because of Dad's firm beliefs, we honored it strictly. We were not even allowed to play in the afternoons when we came home from church, but rather kept the day sacred as best we knew how, mostly in silence and contemplation of what we had heard at church. When other people found out about our custom, some thought us strange. As we grew older, those of us in the family—my older brother Solomon in particular—wondered if they were right.

Dad's ethics were so solid that he became the portrait of righteousness to me. I recognized in him the holiness of God who said, "Be holy, as I am holy." I often saw Dad minister the gospel to people in the streets. But he also did not know how to compromise when compromise was good, and his heightened sense of right and wrong sometimes worked against our family's immediate benefit. During the Second World War, the British army in Palestine deported the Germans who lived in a colony there and seized their belongings. My family badly needed a sewing machine, and among the seized belongings was a fine example of one.

"Here," said the British commander to my father one day (we lived close by), "take this sewing machine. Just give me five pounds, and we'll call it square."

"No," my father said, even though five pounds was nothing for such a superb machine. "That is not yours to give away. It belongs to those Germans."

The commander shrugged and sold the machine to somebody else, to the dismay of the rest of my family who were dreaming of new and repaired clothes.

I RECOGNIZED IN HIM THE HOLINESS OF GOD WHO SAID, "BE HOLY, AS I AM HOLY."

A bit later, our neighbor who worked at the British commissary offered to let Mom buy clothes for us children from the commissary, which was supposed to be for soldiers only. For rock-bottom prices we could have the finest clothing we had ever seen—clothing that would sail through the line of children and hold its stitching as we grew into and out of them. But Dad wouldn't allow it.

"This is wrong and illegal," he said when he heard of it. "I absolutely forbid it."

"Aziz, why are you this way?" Mom shot back, and they sparred most of that day. In the end, though, Mom's practical arguments—which sounded good to us kids—were no match for Dad's principles. He would not budge, and so we dressed in worn pants and torn shirts but had our moral uprightness intact. I was learning an invaluable lesson from my father: how to act honorably in the sight of the Lord, even when others pressured me to cave in.

By the time I was old enough to be aware, the Depression still had not lifted, and our financial situation had not improved. Dad's income was less consistent than ever—up one month, down the next, with frightening droughts that stretched longer than we had imagined possible. His honesty drove him to absorb losses and pay his crew even when an employer cheated him and would not pay. But in those in-between times, God used my mother's brilliance in business to get us through. Mom was clever, smart, diplomatic, and adaptable, like her father. As a young woman, people in her village had called her "sister of men," because she would, when necessary, go to the fields to gather grapes, figs, and fruit and be home by the time the men headed out to the fields to begin working. She took care of her father in his last days and attended to all his properties, which were many.

As a wife and mother, those skills became our family's saving grace, a God-given solution to our poverty. She raised her own chickens, rabbits, and pigeons. While my father insisted we learn the spiritual fundamentals, my mother quietly found ways to put food on the table when we otherwise would have stared at empty plates.

One time, just before the Jewish holy day of Yom Kippur, which involved slaughtering chickens, Mom and I schemed to raise one thousand chicks in our yard, giving them food from the garbage we received at no cost from the nearby army dining room. We kept the chicks warm, fed them the free food, and lost only 10 percent by the time they became adults. Six months after we began, she took a sample chicken to the local rabbi.

"Tell me," he said in amazement. "Are they all as healthy as this one?"

"Healthier," my mother said. He accompanied us to our house and looked over the flock of clucking, scratching hens.

GOD HAD SINGLED ME OUT FOR A
PARTICULAR DESTINY, ONE THAT WOULD
MAKE ME A MARKED MAN AND WOULD
BUILD MY FAITH TO HIGHER LEVELS
THAN I HAD EVER KNOWN.

"You were right," he said after observing them to his satisfaction. "I'll take them all."

With each clever business decision Mom made, I learned about the profound creativity and imagination God uses to overcome problems. Those lessons too would serve me well throughout life.

Meanwhile, Dad kept us on a spiritual regimen, which included family devotions every weeknight. During these times each of us prayed, and while I was still a young boy, praying in front of others was as natural to me as having a normal conversation. One evening when I was ten years old, I had just finished praying when my father pointed his strong, laborer's finger at me and held it there a moment as he prepared to speak. My siblings and mother looked on as I shivered with fear, wondering if I had misspoken in my prayers. Dad's corrections could be fierce, and much of our lives was spent trying to avoid them.

"Son," he said with utter conviction, "God is going to use you to be a minister of the gospel."

The words hit my spirit like lightning. Love for God burst open in me like a flower in springtime, giving me a feeling I had never dreamt possible. Along with it, I suddenly had a strong desire to win people to Christ. Those two things, I felt, would guide my life from that moment forth. I went to my room and lay in my bed and let the strange and wondrous feelings wash over me as nightfall came over the city outside my window. From that moment forward I would never be without those desires to preach the gospel and win souls, but I would soon realize that the promise also made me a greater target of the enemy. God had singled me out for a particular destiny, one that would make me a marked man and would build my faith to higher levels than I had ever known.

My newfound spirituality earned me a reputation with my brothers. They nicknamed me "the prophet" and would ask me to predict when our father was coming home from work on those days when he was late. I would tell them when I thought he would return, and I was usually correct, to their continued amazement. I enjoyed a closeness with God for several years and never missed Sunday school or church, both of which I enjoyed immensely. I felt that God was feeding me by hand as a parent feeds a child. Life was simple and uncomplicated, and I was mercifully shielded from outer influences that might have stolen my love for Christ. My faith began to grow from a seedling into a sturdy tree.

But as I became a teenager, I became aware of my surroundings and of life beyond my father's jurisdiction. Growing up in our house was like growing up in a windowless room through whose walls one can hear the revelries and celebrations of irreligious people on the other side having a terrific time. Dad never allowed us to do "worldly" things: we had no radio, and going to the movies was tantamount to stepping into hell's foyer. Instead, our lives were full of prayer and Bible reading, which had satisfied me for a while, but now seemed pale compared to the "fun" I thought everyone else was having. A rebellious weed grew up in my heart and began to choke out my loyalty to Jesus. I began to resist the path I knew God had chosen for me. I desired to experience forbidden things, to see what was on the other side of that wall—to live, just for a while, the way the world lived.

I left St. Luke's, the Anglican mission school where I had attended grade school, and went on to high school where I took a whole raft of classes—chemistry, biology, algebra, and geometry, all in the English language. The only thing I disliked more than some of the subjects were the instructors themselves, and soon my boredom, combined with my emerging leadership abilities, led me into serious mischief. I didn't like chemistry and biology class, so I rallied the others to join me in harassing the teacher. Several other kids and I went to class prepared with a supply of rubber bands and orange peels, and, when he turned his back to write formulas on the chalkboard, we shot a fusillade of orange peels at the back of his head with the rubber bands—*thunk!* I had never done anything quite so daring or (we thought) hilarious, but in our over-zealousness to impress each other and our classmates, we sent up one too many orange-peel volleys! No battle plan goes exactly as planned, and this time we got caught. Because the instructor identified me as the ringleader, I was sent to the principal's office.

FOR THE FIRST TIME AS A YOUNG MAN, I KNEW WHAT IT WAS TO BE CORRECTED WITH LOVE.

"Elias, are you really doing the things the teacher told me you were?" Reverend Hooper asked me. He was the school's principal, or headmaster, as we called him. He was an Englishman and an Anglican minister, tall and slender, calm, cool, and unflappable. Fear cascaded over my heart as I looked into his honest eyes. He seemed the human portrait of integrity. Suddenly I heard myself denying the accusations and lying boldly.

"I didn't do anything wrong," I said, surprised at my own words echoing off the walls of his office. I said them with so much conviction, I could hardly believe it was me talking. I marveled at my willingness to deceive. Where had I learned it? I didn't know.

He looked me over a bit skeptically.

"OK," he said. "You say you didn't do it. I believe you. You can go back to class."

I turned and left the office, feeling gluttonous with victory and drunk with the lie. Reverend Hooper, on the other hand, seemed quietly confident that time would prove whether I had told him the truth or not. A few days later, emboldened by my narrow escape, my sense of adventure flared up again, and I was caught disrupting class. This time Reverend Hooper did not ask me whether I was guilty or not. He came out from behind his desk and stood before me.

"Elias," he said, "you need some help, and I want to help you because I love you. Please bend over and touch your toes without bending your knees."

I could not believe what was happening. I was fifteen years old—and yet this preacher took a cane, drew his hand back, and whacked me severely on my posterior. I jumped at the shock of it, and the pain. He looked at me, smiling.

"You need that. Please bend over again."

I bent over, and he caned me again. My eyes misted over from the sting and the humiliation.

"This is good for you. Bend over again," he said.

I bent over a third time, and he gave me a final, brisk spanking. Then he stood me up, turned me around, and hugged me.

"I could have expelled you from school," he said, "but because I love you, I did what I did."

He patted me on the shoulder, and I went back to class, grateful that no one else had to know what I had gone through. The pain of that caning seemed to stay with me for a lifetime, but I eventually learned that it was good pain— pain that guided me away from distracting "adventures" and kept me on a right path. I never misbehaved in that class again. For the first time as a young man, I knew what it was to be corrected with love. Reverend Hooper knew the power of godly discipline, and he had used it well on me.

My brother Solomon, meanwhile, felt he had outgrown my father's rules. He was four years older than me, my hero, and already a veteran of the Jordanian army at age twenty-one. Of all the Malki children, he was the smartest and most handsome, but he began to set a bad example for me and the others. He flouted Dad's wishes and began gambling and womanizing. He and my father fought like tigers when they were both home, and soon Solomon ran away to escape my father's authority. Suddenly there were two paths before us: the way of our father and Solomon's way. To a teenager like me, Solomon's way promised freedom and adventure, and so I began patterning my life after his. As my mind shifted in that direction, my father's ways seemed increasingly antiquated and stiff. At night I would think of Solomon's bravery as he struck out on his own. I envisioned him having a grand old time on the town while I was cooped up in our house where nothing ever happened.

Palestine was becoming more dangerous by the day as the civil war between the Jews and the British heated up. My family decided to move back to Lebanon in 1947, but instead of feeling like a homecoming, we felt like a caravan of strangers returning to a vaguely familiar land. The small, poor city of Beirut was crowded with refugees from the war in Palestine. We stayed with my uncle for a few months, sharing a single outdoor toilet with five families, then finally found a two-bedroom apartment to rent. By now I had ten brothers and sisters. Since we were a big family, my father needed us boys—John, Solomon, David, and I—to work to help support our younger siblings. I never finished high school but became a carpenter for Dad in his construction job. Solomon worked for him, too, but less regularly and always with a defiance I found increasingly admirable.

I PERFORMED EACH OF THESE WITH
SPECIAL CARE, HOPING TO REVIVE MY
HERO, TO PLAY SOME PART IN THE
DASHING, DRAMATIC STORY OF HIS LIFE.

The streets of Beirut were alive with Ford automobiles in those days, and they served as public transportation. If you wanted to go downtown, you found four other people to share a Ford with you, and together you paid the driver a quarter. The streets were a cacophony of honking horns, bicycles, and people selling fruits and vegetables of widely varying quality. I got to know the scene well when, quite suddenly, Solomon became very ill. His sickness was a mystery to us and to the doctors. For two months Dad and I ferried him back and forth to the hospital through streets crammed with poverty-stricken refugees, and Solomon suffered greatly. When the doctors reached the limits of what they could do, they sent him home weakened and dying.

I cared for him personally in my parents' room, which was converted to a sickroom. No longer could I dream of the adventures he was having in the world beyond our home. Now he lay before me unable to care for himself in the simplest of ways. We took turns feeding him, sponging him with water, and emptying his bedpan. I performed each of these with special care, hoping to revive my hero, to play some part in the dashing, dramatic story of his life. I was standing by his bed one day with my aunt when Solomon took two clipped, labored breaths, then gave up his spirit. His body went limp. His eyes stopped moving beneath their eyelids. He lay as still as a half-empty sack of grain. My aunt screamed; Mom ran in from outside. Solomon was dead.

We had to bury him that same day because there was nowhere to keep the body. Dad called the Presbyterian pastor and arranged the funeral, and that afternoon my family followed the men who bore Solomon's casket on their shoulders on a forty-minute procession to the Presbyterian cemetery. As we walked solemnly through the streets, people stood back and gave us their respectful silence. At the cemetery the preacher said a few words and read from the Scriptures. I stood there in shock, knowing that if death had taken Solomon, it could take me just as easily.

In Solomon's death, God was graciously calling me back to the faith I had considered abandoning.

⁓

Sadness overshadowed us in the following months, and my own spiritual struggle became more urgent. Suddenly, life on the other side of the wall did not seem the jubilant escape I had pictured it when I was shuttered up in my parents' home. As Solomon's light had dimmed, so too the world had lost its luster to me.

I began to consider my life more fully, and my questions kept leading me to Christ. I remembered my experience as a ten-year-old boy, as if rediscovering an old, buried treasure. I felt a strong desire to ask Him into my life for good and to experience the transformation it would bring, but I did not know how, and there was no one, not even at our church, to lead me in the sinner's prayer. One time at another church a Sunday school teacher, who was a born-again Christian, offered to pray with me to accept Christ. I took the offer. But by the time I got out of church, nothing felt different, and I was easily pulled back to the world's dismal promises. For several years after Solomon's death my heart was divided in two. I knew enough to realize that when you gave yourself to Christ, there was no going back, but in my young, foolish mind I was convinced I should wait and see if the world had anything better to offer. Perhaps Solomon had been right after all. And if I committed my life to Christ it would have to be forever. I would rather have been a sinner than a backslider.

I kept going to the Presbyterian church and even joined the youth group and took the oath they required, but I still lacked the transformation of being born again. I had knowledge of Christ in my head, but I resisted His control of my heart. Instead, I was splitting time between church and my friends who were Christians in name only. I had picked up their worldly habits, which were forbidden in my father's household: card playing ("a tool for gambling," he always said), going to shows, and joining clubs—activities Solomon had relished and Dad found unthinkable.

I followed my father into the contracting business, and with enthusiasm and a lot of hustle I began to find success. I put together my own crew, and we worked jobs around town. I discovered I was good at dealing with property owners who had hired us. I enjoyed working hard and seeing the fruits of my labor, and after completing a couple of jobs I realized I was on my way to making a good deal of money. Even though I was only eighteen, I was hiring and paying wages to men who were much older than me. My career looked promising, and I saw it as a way to escape the poverty that had dogged my family.

I BEGAN TO CONSIDER MY LIFE MORE FULLY, AND MY QUESTIONS KEPT LEADING ME TO CHRIST.

Then one day toward the end of the year when I was just shy of nineteen years old, an acquaintance came to me and said, "Some Americans are living nearby and having church in their home. Would you like to go with me to their meeting?"

"Sure," I said, not thinking much of it, and I attended their Christmas celebration. I enjoyed myself tremendously. There was a purity and joy unlike any I had found in secular entertainment. Instead of rules I found freedom and love, both of which made me almost dizzy. I decided to attend their New Year's Eve meeting as well, but in the intervening week I forgot about my commitment and instead found myself playing cards with my cousin and his friends on the last night of the year. They were teaching me new games, new ways to gamble, when the clock struck midnight and the bells rang out. Suddenly I remembered my promise to the missionaries. I felt awful.

"I've got to go," I told my compatriots.

"Why?" they said. "You are just getting good."

I stood up and made for the door.

"I told people I'd go to their party, and I don't want to let them down," I said. They shrugged and turned back to their game. I made the fifteen-minute walk to the missionaries' home to apologize, but when I got there the party was over. Guests poured into the street, hugging each other and saying good-byes and Happy New Years.

"I'm sorry for missing the meeting," I told one of the leaders, feeling abashed and sinful.

"That's OK," he said. "We will see you next Sunday."

"OK," I said, and this time I was determined to keep my word. On that first Sunday of 1951 I came to their home and for the first time in my life heard a woman preacher, Dr. Flora Colby. I had never met anyone like her. She was forty years old and had beautiful blue eyes. She had the habit of walking straight and fast wherever she needed to go, and she would give anything she owned to someone in need. She worked as a chiropractor and ran a clinic in town. In her spare time she rode horses, played the accordion and the guitar, and was a persuasive and powerful preacher of the full gospel.

She preached so convincingly that day about the Second Coming of Christ that I felt I was in the very presence of God. My faith revived, the Holy Spirit opened my heart, and the love of God invaded my life with full force. At the end of the service I was so sure of my destiny and so excited about getting there, that I walked confidently down to the altar area, knelt, and said, "Yes, Lord, I will serve You with all my heart and give up the world." The words sounded true, as if they were ringing through the halls of heaven. I had never felt anything so wonderful.

God had intervened and changed the direction of my life, and I could not ignore His call.

But when I looked down into the street from that second-floor balcony, I saw two young men below—gang leaders who routinely caused trouble for the missionaries. I knew they would start a fight with me when I went down. I turned to Dr. Colby's husband, Ralph, a butcher by profession, and said, "Could you walk with me until we pass those men?" He agreed, and when we got to the first floor the two men tried to cause trouble for me, but they couldn't because Ralph was with me. He walked about a block with me and then turned back, and I took off for home, running through the streets of Beirut. I felt I was being borne up on the clouds. My heart soared into the night sky with happiness, and I realized that I had been yearning for years to know that my sins were forgiven—and now I knew they were.

The whole world was new when I awoke the next morning. Everything looked beautiful, crisp, clear, and alive. I headed to my job as a contractor, but I knew that this construction project would be my last. No matter how much success I was having, it was time to lay aside my career pursuits and follow the calling God had revealed to me when I was a boy. God had intervened and changed the direction of my life, and I could not ignore His call.

I went to Dr. Colby and asked, "What can I do for Jesus?" She promptly turned me into her song leader, Sunday school teacher, youth leader, and director of the Easter and Christmas plays. For four days a week I volunteered at the small mission church and became the spiritual leader of the young people. My life was an example to those who had been raised in nominal Christian households but did not know about the born-again experience. The Lord developed my gift of leadership, and as I put my faith into practice He gave me more responsibilities. I taught Sunday school, using all the Bible knowledge I had gained from my father's nightly Bible studies. When Christmas and Easter rolled around I produced two shows with a wonderful cast of actors who portrayed the Christmas and Easter stories. We gave spirited performances.

But before long, I faced strong opposition that would test my commitment to the path I had chosen to follow. But as the tests came, so did greater faith, and I knew God was preparing me for glorious ministry in the Middle East.

Chapter 3

AN AMERICAN JOURNEY

I TRIED TO KEEP my feet beneath me on the storm-tossed freight ship, the SS *Neahellas*, positioned somewhere in the Atlantic Ocean between Europe and North America. The winds and waves had grown so violent that I, and the three dozen people on board, had lapsed into sober contemplation, wondering if we would lose our lives. There was nothing we could do. The gargantuan freighter groaned under the strain of the storm, launching upward under the propulsion of a giant swell, then diving like a rocket into the next trough. With the exception of myself, everyone on board—including the captain—had fallen seasick. I made my way room to room, bringing the passengers and crew water with which to wash themselves. As they moaned and rolled about on their beds, I cleaned up after them. The floor pitched beneath me like a trampoline.

But though I escaped seasickness, my own personal tempest was about to begin. After a week, the storm outside quieted and ship life returned to normal—a dull progression of days as we waited to make landfall in New York City. One day I was eating in the dining room, taking my time, when the purser called me to his office.

<hr/>

DURING THOSE MONTHS I DEVELOPED A YEARNING TO TRAIN FOR FULL-TIME MINISTRY.

<hr/>

"You have a telex from Beirut, Lebanon, from your brother John Malki," he said, and handed me the paper. It read:

> Watch out. You are in trouble. Dr. Colby is on her way by plane to New York to meet you. Do not talk to her. Carry on with your itinerary and go to California. She said she is going to tell the authorities not to let you in the country. After you left a lot of trouble took place. People were gossiping, and they accused you of some things and she believed it.
>
> —YOUR BROTHER, JOHN

The words pierced my heart like an arrow shot all the way from Beirut. Tremors of sadness and panic went through me. Dr. Colby had been instrumental in helping me gain passage and permission to go to America to attend

Bible school. What had happened in my absence? Could John's message be true? If only I could have spoken with him face-to-face and learned more! My mind ran back and forth, believing and then dismissing the message. Losing Dr. Colby's support was too devastating to consider; it was like losing the support of a parent. But I could not discount John's message, which he must have sent with great difficulty and expense. I was churned up inside like the seas had been days before. I took the message to my cabin, knelt down at my little bed, and cried out to the Lord.

As I prayed, my mind scrutinized every detail of the months leading up to my departure. After coming to the Lord I had thrown myself into ministry work in Lebanon. Dr. Colby had used me well, and I was a one-man labor force doing everything I could to support her church. Then I took a paying job as a field representative for the *Lutheran Hour* radio program, which broadcast for half an hour, once a week from Monte Carlo. My duty was to sign up people to study the life of Christ and the life of the apostle Paul by correspondence. I tackled the work with gusto, traveling by foot, car, and bus to visit people in their homes. Such was my zeal that in one year I visited one thousand villages in Lebanon and led many people to Jesus. Not a day or night went by that I didn't work myself to near exhaustion.

During those months I developed a yearning to train for full-time ministry. I knew I would need to be well-equipped in Bible study if I were to have any effect on the Middle East. God had put a big vision in my heart for reaching the Middle Eastern people—Arabs and Jews—with the gospel, though I did not know how I would accomplish this. All I knew was that my first step was to find a Bible school and learn all I could.

But to my knowledge, there was no full gospel Bible school in all the Middle East. I spoke about my desire with Dr. Colby, my mentor and encourager. She was touched and wrote to a small Bible school she knew of in Gilroy, California, asking them to accept me. Within a few weeks the principal there sent an acceptance letter, and I rejoiced. Armed with his invitation to attend, Dr. Colby and I went to the embassy in Beirut to secure a visa for me.

"GOD MADE IT CLEAR I WOULD TAKE THE GOSPEL TO THE MIDDLE EAST.... I WON'T LET MY FAITH BE SHAKEN."

The American consulate, a man named William Shockley, asked me a few questions and quickly granted me the visa, stamping my passport and handing me a complete student package, which allowed me to study in California. I had four months to use the visa, and if I did not, the visa would expire. When Dr. Colby and I left the office I was flushed with excitement.

"All I need now is the four hundred dollars to buy a ticket to the United States," I told her.

"That may be a bigger hurdle than you imagine," she said. "You need to pray and get to work on it."

"I will," I said with naïve confidence. "It won't be a problem at all."

I made only thirty-three dollars a month with the *Lutheran Hour*—just enough to cover my monthly living expenses. I no longer held my job as a contractor, and our family remained poor; four hundred dollars was well beyond what we could scrape together, even if all of us pitched in. My brothers John and David worked. The younger children were still in school. But I had no idea how to tackle the challenge of raising money, so I prayed for miraculous provision. None came. The days slipped away like sand in an hourglass, and sooner than I expected the four months passed. I had failed to gather even close to what I needed for passage. My visa expired, and I went to Dr. Colby, crestfallen. She and Ralph comforted me, and I took their advice and would not allow myself to question my calling.

"God made it clear I would take the gospel to the Middle East," I said through tears. "I have a commission. I won't let my faith be shaken."

As I reassured myself, in the back of my mind I thought of my grandfather who had stood firm in his goal right to the end of his life. I thought of my father, who had remained faithful to the Lord through many hardships. They were faithful, and I could be faithful in my generation, too. Yes, I had exhausted my resources in trying to go through this particular door, but it would not be the only door. I gathered my thoughts and regrouped. Over the following weeks, I did the practical thing and forgot about visas and ocean passages and Bible schools in the United States. I told myself that God would establish me in ministry some other way—I just had to wait and see how.

But my hopes were rekindled when Nicholas, one of the young men in the church who had the money to buy a ticket, acquired acceptance papers from the same school in Gilroy with Dr. Colby's help. When I learned of this, I went to Dr. Colby with renewed fire.

"God will help me get the money if you write the school again and ask for an up-to-date acceptance letter," I said confidently.

"Elias," she said, "I hate to see you get hurt. Why don't you forget about it? You don't have the money."

But I would not give up. Other missionaries, whom I called Mr. and Mrs. Meyers, arrived in Lebanon, and they knew the president of the school to which I had applied. I was helping them in their work, and when I explained my situation, they helped me secure a fresh acceptance letter. In the meantime, Dr. Colby had written the school on behalf of Nicholas, who suddenly seemed to have favored status in our Christian community.

My letter of acceptance arrived before his, and I asked Dr. Colby to accompany me again to the American embassy to renew my visa. This time she did not want to, and her husband counseled against it, but I felt that she should go with me.

"Pray with me," I told them, "and make up your minds when we have finished."

We prayed, and when we finished she looked at me and said, "I will go with you." Across town we went again to see Mr. Shockley.

"You didn't go already?" he said when he saw me. Then without any questions he stamped my passport and renewed my visa for four more months. I was elated, but I faced the same impossible task of raising money. This time I would not be so passive.

The following week Dr. Colby received a letter of acceptance for Nicholas, and everyone we knew was excited for him. But when they went to see the consulate for a visa, he gave them bad news, which then carried over to me. I learned of it when I saw Nicholas and Dr. Colby hanging around church with long faces.

I WAS BAPTIZED IN THE COOL, CLEAR WATERS THERE, AND I FINALLY FELT COMPLETE BECAUSE I HAD OBEYED THE LORD'S COMMAND.

"Mr. Shockley told me to give you a message," she said. "He made a mistake. The school in Gilroy is not registered to accept foreign students. When we went yesterday to get a visa for Nicholas, the consulate looked at the book and could not find the school's name. That means your visa is not really valid. When you get to the border they will send you back. He already told Washington about it, and he said to tell you not to travel."

I could hardly have received more bitter news. Why would God have given me a visa twice if He didn't want me to go to America? In my heart, I saw beyond the consulate, beyond the visa, and I knew that in spite of laws that might stand in the way, I was to attend Bible school in America. I prayed desperately for the money so I could make passage with my questionable visa, but nothing happened. I tried to borrow money from Nicholas, but he refused me. Still, I would not give up.

Then, out of the blue, my uncle on my mother's side came to see us one day. He had inherited all of my grandfather's money and the many properties my grandfather had owned. One particular piece of property was still in my grandfather's name, thirty years after his death. My uncle wanted to build on the property but needed the signatures of all the living children—including my mother.

"Listen," I advised Mom, appealing to her business savvy. "Don't sign unless he pays you enough to help me."

She agreed, and named the price for her signature when my uncle came by to negotiate. He agreed to give her some money, but not enough to buy my ticket. She had done the best she could, but my visa deadline crept closer, and I still had no prospect for making up the gap. I continued to pray and to work for the Lord. Then, abruptly, my brother John was laid off from the job he had held for several years. We received this as bad news at first, but then we learned that according to Lebanese law, he was entitled to a nice sum of retirement money. Knowing my need and my desperate desire, John generously offered me the money, which I combined with my mother's inheritance. Now I had enough to go to America. That night my praises rang loud to God for supplying what I had been unable to supply on my own.

I bought a ticket for ocean passage to New York City. I was scheduled to leave Lebanon on October 6, 1952, five days after my twenty-first birthday. But one thing still troubled me: I was not yet baptized in water. My father, a Presbyterian, believed in sprinkling, and as any respectful child in the Middle East would do, I had chosen not to offend him by being baptized by immersion until he approved. But on the day of my departure I worked up the courage to force his hand a little.

"Dad, I would like to be baptized in water before I leave, and I want you to be present," I said. "Would you approve of it and go with me?"

He hemmed and hawed for a moment but couldn't say no, so I called Mr. and Mrs. Meyers. Together with my parents and siblings, we took a minibus to Abraham's River, an hour north of Beirut. I was baptized in the cool, clear waters there, and I finally felt complete because I had obeyed the Lord's command. Within hours we had driven back to the pier, and a host of friends and well-wishers, including Dr. Colby and many people from the church, stood by to bid me farewell. Before I boarded, we prayed together that God would do great and mighty things, showing himself strong in my life as He had done by helping me buy a ticket. My mother cried, and so did I as I waved to them from the deck.

So, to receive the troubling telex from John two weeks later while I was cooped up on a lonely freighter in threatening seas threw me into bewilderment and deep sadness. There in my little cabin I knelt on the floor, opened my Bible, and asked the Lord to give me a verse to encourage me. My eyes fell on Joshua 1:5, to which my Bible was already open:

> There shall not any man be able to stand before thee all the days of thy life: as I was with Moses, so I will be with thee: I will not fail thee, nor forsake thee.

I got up from where I was kneeling and praised the Lord, my voice echoing off the steel walls and down the lonely corridor. Peace poured into my soul like the sunlight pouring onto the ship's deck outside, and I knew that whatever happened, all would be well. Dr. Colby might try to hinder me, the immigration officers might try to stop me, but somehow God would make a way. His ultimate purpose in my life would be accomplished.

Finally, on November 2, 1952, twenty-seven days after the voyage began, we arrived at New York harbor. It was two days before the presidential election between Dwight D. Eisenhower and Adlai Stevenson, and the country was abuzz with anticipation. Passengers began disembarking our freighter, grateful for the sight of solid ground, but my steps were a bit more cautious. More than once I caught my breath, waiting to see the face of Dr. Colby in the crowd of people on the massive pier. I didn't know what I would do if she tried to interfere, so I built up my courage and walked steadily on to where an immigration officer was seated at a desk.

"Have your papers ready," he barked, and people clutched their all-important documents. He checked each person's papers. I could feel the excitement and energy of America wafting over me, as if optimism were part of the very air. I knew that if God allowed me to stay I would learn great things that would shape my life forever.

The line moved forward, and people passed through one by one until it was my turn. I handed the officer a manila envelope with all my documents, and after looking them over he glanced at me skeptically.

"Please stand to the side," he said without bothering to tell me why.

Other passengers continued to pass through, but I was not allowed to move beyond him. Finally, when every other person I had sailed with on those unpredictable seas had been allowed to enter the country, blending into the city like bees drawn to a hive, the officer turned to me.

"You are under arrest and will be detained because your papers are not in order," he said. "The school that invited you to the United States is not registered to accept foreign students. I'm sorry. You'll have to come with me."

AS I PRAYED, I TOLD HIM MY DESIRES, AND THEN I LEFT IT TO HIM TO DO WHATEVER HE WANTED.

I could say nothing in response. I had traveled thousands of miles and run into a wall. He led me down the empty runway, and then I saw Dr. Colby standing on the platform. She looked so out of place there, alone but self-contained and confident as always. In spite of the warning I had received from my brother John, I felt a surge of love for her. She had been such a friend to me back in Beirut. I also felt a stab of pain because apparently John had been right: she had come all the way to America to stop me, for reasons I didn't fully understand. I descended the runway step by step, and our eyes passed but did not meet. As we walked by, she leaned in and asked the immigration officer, "Where are they taking that young man?"

"Ellis Island," he said. "He'll be detained there."

That was all I heard. Dr. Colby had traveled across the ocean, but her trip had been useless. I was already in detention, and her purpose had been accomplished by fastidious American bureaucrats. The officers put me on a ferry, and soon I landed on Ellis Island and was escorted to a large dormitory with thirty beds.

"This is your bed," the officer told me, pointing to one of the bunks. Then he left me alone.

I looked around at my new home. Other beds looked well-used. Some were made. Some were not. Some had people sleeping on them in the middle of the day. Many had luggage, bags, and personal items beneath them. I slid my suitcases under my bed, which was hardly more than a cot.

"God, how long will I be here?" I prayed silently. I was in an in-between world, a noncountry. I was on U.S. soil, breathing U.S. air, but I may as well have been tucked away in a prison.

After a while, I struck up a conversation with other detainees and learned that some had been there for two months, some for six months, some for two years. I couldn't imagine staying in limbo that long.

"You can't do anything to speed things up," one of them said. "You might as well enjoy the stay."

I knew that if God wanted me in America, He would have to make a way. As it was, they would probably want to deport me, but I had no money to make passage back to Beirut. And even if by some extraordinary grace I was permitted to stay, Dr. Colby was there to fight against me. Slowly, I began to see that I might never fulfill my dream of training for ministry in America. Perhaps God had another plan for me, and this was a long detour. As I prayed, I told Him my desires, and then I left it to Him to do whatever He wanted. I knew He had called me to minister in the Middle East; I would cooperate with Him, however He chose to fulfill that promise.

The days of waiting seemed endless, but I made a significant discovery. There was a flickering box in the hallway. For twenty-five cents you could watch images on it for thirty minutes before it shut off. One day somebody put a quarter in, and it jumped to life, emitting noise and displaying moving pictures on its glass. I watched in amazement, but I didn't know what it was. For the first time in my life I was looking at a television. I had no clue as I stared at it that the novel device would play a major part in my ministry.

Four days after I arrived, my case came up, and I was called to appear before the judge. With no ceremony whatsoever, I was escorted into a courtroom where a judge sat at a bench, the American flag hanging behind him and officers standing to the side. I stood before him as he shuffled through my papers, absorbing the details. Then he looked up at me with surprising compassion.

"We are very sorry, but we cannot let you go to California because the school you want to attend is not registered to accept foreign students," he said. "You must go back home."

"I don't have any money to get back home," I said. I had rehearsed this conversation in my mind for days.

"Then you have to find another school to accept you," he said.

"I don't know of any other school," I replied, hoping perhaps that they had a list I could choose from—a place to which I could appeal.

"Then the only solution is for you to find an American citizen who is willing to sponsor you as a visitor for six months," he said. "Then you can go to the school in Gilroy for six months, and when the six months are over you must go to a different school that can accept foreign students."

I considered his words for a moment. I knew nobody in the entire country. He could have given me a dozen free phone calls, and it still would not have helped me. Every door was closing. But God was still on my side, I was sure. My faith had not diminished, but had grown stronger than ever.

"I don't know anyone here," I finally admitted.

He leaned back for a moment and looked at me.

"There is an American lady outside in the hallway who said she knows you," he said. "She came and inquired about you. Maybe she will help you."

He could only have meant Dr. Colby, but I was surprised to hear she was still in the country. *What if I allow her in?* I thought. She might, in her eloquence, blacken my name with the immigration authorities forever, convincing them to never allow me into the U.S. She might fill the room with accusations that had been building inside her ever since the mysterious misunderstanding took place in Beirut. I weighed the risk. I did not want to involve her, but what other options did I have? A known enemy in a strange land seemed better than having nobody at all.

And perhaps God would intervene in some unexpected way on my behalf. Faith rose up within me. I felt like Joseph of the Bible stuck in prison, waiting to be free. Just as Joseph had received a miracle at the right time, I was counting on God to chart out my steps according to His plan. I knew the answer lay not with Dr. Colby or with the judge or the bailiffs, but with God.

I looked up at the judge and said, "Please call her in."

He nodded and motioned to an officer who disappeared into the hallway, and a moment later Dr. Colby stepped into the room. It was so odd to be in an Ellis Island detention hearing with her, when the last time we had been together at any length was at a pier on the Mediterranean Sea.

"You inquired about this man's case," the judge said. "He needs an American who will sign an affidavit of support for him for six months."

JUST AS JOSEPH HAD RECEIVED A
MIRACLE AT THE RIGHT TIME, I WAS
COUNTING ON GOD TO CHART OUT MY
STEPS ACCORDING TO HIS PLAN.

She looked at me and then at the judge. I could not read her face, what she would say, why she had come. I waited, holding my breath, wondering what direction God would send me—east or west?

"I will be happy to sign an affidavit of support for Elias," she said. She stepped forward, signed the paper, and I was suddenly free to enter the United States. The impossible had taken place right before my eyes.

We walked together from the room and into a hallway. I carried my bags; she walked briskly and with confidence, as always. I felt a surge of elation at my approaching freedom. Each step seemed lighter than the one before.

"Aren't you surprised to see me here?" she said.

"Yes, I am," I replied. "Why did you come?"

She spoke as we made our way to the ferry platform. I could see the magnificent skyline of New York City on the other side of the Hudson Bay, a postcard portrait come to life. I was about to walk right into it.

"When you left Lebanon, people told me you were saying bad things about me," she said. "I believed them, and I didn't want that kind of person representing me in the United States and in the Bible school. So I came here to do everything in my power to stop you. But when I saw you four days ago at the pier, and you were already detained by the government, I went to a hotel and sought the Lord as to why I was here. An angel of the Lord appeared to me and said that I should not do anything to hurt you. On the contrary, he said the Lord brought me from Lebanon to America because He knew you would need someone to sponsor you as I did today. He said all the gossip I had heard in Lebanon was a lie and that you are a man of God."

She paused a moment. In the distance a ship blew its horn, and I heard the cry of seagulls and the clink-clank of barge chains mingled with the shouts of the vessels' crews. Dr. Colby looked at me with a big smile and eyes brimming with faith.

"God is going to use you greatly in the Middle East, Elias," she said. "God's ways are not our ways. I had to borrow the money for my air ticket to come here. If God had told me I was coming to help you, I would never have come. But you are God's man. He will use you."

Relief washed over me. God had worked out every detail of my immigration in advance, doing what I could not have done even with my best planning. We took the ferry to New York, and for the first time I ate in an American restaurant. When Dr. Colby told the waitress she wanted a hot dog, I blurted out, "You mean you eat dogs in this country?"

Dr. Colby laughed and laughed until I thought she wouldn't recover. I laughed, too, and then she explained what a hot dog was. By that time I felt so lighthearted that I knew no matter what challenges lay ahead, God would make a way— even if it took many miracles.

And, as I was soon to find out, it would take many miracles indeed.

Chapter 4

LIFE CHANGES

THE TWELVE-SEAT PROPELLER plane hopscotched across the country from New York to San Francisco, stopping to refuel, then taking off again. The flight was long, but nothing like the ocean passage I had survived. As I looked out the window at the great country passing below me, I knew this journey was the next step to reaching a dream I desperately wanted to fulfill: I longed to become a missionary to the Middle East, no matter what dangers that entailed. I wanted to follow the path my grandfather had pioneered so bravely. But there would be obstacles to overcome on the way there.

A Greyhound bus picked me up at the San Francisco airport and deposited me in Gilroy, California, a small town in the golden foothills twenty miles from the Pacific Ocean. Gilroy was the garlic capital of the world—a fact I quickly discerned because of the pungent scent of fresh garlic that permeated the city day and night. The odor was inescapable, and eventually it became as familiar to me as the feel of my own clothes.

The Bible school I had enrolled in was the kind of place my father had warned me against—a place for fanatics and "holy rollers." As a devoted Presbyterian, Dad only went to church for an hour at a time, and there was no funny business—no loud singing or clapping, no shouting, no kneeling. When I arrived at the Bible school, I couldn't see what he had been concerned about. The place seemed tame enough. A young man greeted me and led me to my dorm where I would live with fifteen other young men. I brought my suitcase in and set it on my bunk then had a look around campus. It was simple enough: a cluster of buildings, a courtyard, a parking lot. But at chapel service the next day I was suddenly introduced to a kind of Pentecostalism I had never seen. People clapped their hands, danced around the room, and rolled on the floor. I was bug-eyed with amazement, even as I tried to join in. At the Pentecostal mission church in Lebanon we had never behaved like that. I sang along and tried not to look too surprised by it all, and by the second week I noticed my hands were sore and tired. I had never clapped so much in my life.

The students and instructors were exuberant about worship, but they were even more exhilarated about the baptism of the Holy Spirit, which my father opposed as well. One night back in Lebanon I had attended a meeting at the Pentecostal mission church where we prayed until 1:00 a.m., with some people receiving the baptism. I didn't receive the baptism that night, but when I went home and Dad learned where I had been and what I had been doing, he cornered me on the balcony of the fourth-floor apartment we lived in at the time.

"If you don't quit going to that mission I am going to throw you off the balcony," he said, face hot with anger.

"Dad," I said, swallowing my fear, "I am going to go to the mission church, so if you want to throw me off the balcony, here I am. You might as well do it now."

He looked at me squarely and saw I was determined to go. He walked into the apartment and never brought up the subject again.

NOW I KNEW WHAT ALL THE FUSS HAD
BEEN ABOUT, AND I DETERMINED TO
MAKE THIS AMAZING EXPERIENCE A
CORNERSTONE OF MY MINISTRY.

Now at the American Bible school, teachers and fellow students approached me at every service to pray for me to receive the baptism. They gripped my shoulders and shook me, prayed and shouted to God on my behalf, massaged my shoulders and neck, and exhorted me to receive it. Strangely, no one ever took the time to sit down in sober fashion and teach me about the baptism in the Holy Spirit, though my mind thirsted for answers about what the Bible said it was and what it would do for me. I underwent many sessions where fellow students and instructors tried to induce the baptism in me through this variety of methods, and I soon grew tired of suffering under their experimentations. The baptism remained a mystery, though one I sincerely desired.

Then one night a friend was playing his guitar in our dorm room, and we were all singing praise songs to God. Suddenly we became happy—happier than we would have been naturally. Some people got up and walked around the room with their hands raised. Others clapped and shouted. I remained sitting, but I felt deeply content and full of joy. Some friends began to pray for me, and before I knew what was happening, I hit the floor, opened my mouth, and began to speak in a language I had never learned.

I SHARED WITH HER THAT I WAS GOING
TO BE A MISSIONARY TO THE MIDDLE
EAST. SHE TOLD ME THAT GOD HAD
CALLED HER TO BE A MISSIONARY, TOO.

"He got it! He got it!" they said, dancing around. As their feet clomped around on the ground near my head, I continued to speak in tongues, feeling the waterfall of joy flowing through me. I had never known that such glory was available to people. Now I knew what all the fuss had been about, and I determined to make this amazing experience a cornerstone of my ministry.

But then, as our impromptu praise meeting came to a close, I began to doubt what had just happened to me. Nobody had explained to me what had happened and why. I had no framework for how the baptism and my new prayer language fit into my life, how it supplemented my work for Christ, or how I should maintain the gift God had given to me. My mind swirled with questions, just as it had been caught up in wonder moments before. Laying in bed that night, I speculated that I had made the whole thing up. Maybe Dad was right that the Pentecostal experience was a distraction, a group delusion, a side road away from the pure gospel. I woke up with this same tug-of-war in my mind, but word had spread about what had happened to me. At the request of my instructors, I shared about the experience in chapel service. There were great cheers and applause and praise from my fellow students, but I didn't mention my doubts. Rather, I pondered the experience in my heart and waited, hoping God would send someone to instruct me about it.

My time in Gilroy was necessarily limited to six months because of my visa. I had supported myself by pumping gas at a nearby gas station. (With the extra, I saved enough to buy my first car, a used 1946 Chevrolet Coupe, which I then traded for a 1948 Studebaker.) In the spring of 1953, as the days left on my visa ticked away, I accepted invitations to speak in churches and share my testimony. One invitation was from a youth conference in Big Bear, California, eight hours away in southern California. I made the long drive and spoke to the people there about what God had done in my life.

Something unexpected happened during that week. I met Donna Allen. She was there with many of her girlfriends, but I thought she alone was the most beautiful girl in the camp. I learned she had been saved on October 6, 1952—the day I left Lebanon. I shared with her that I was going to be a missionary to the Middle East. She told me that God had called her to be a missionary, too. I was smitten by her and would never recover. I had only a few days to win her, and she didn't make it easy, but after a while she began to pay attention to me.

I returned to Gilroy, and we kept in touch, but by then my student visa had expired, and I did not have legal status in the United States. The immigration authorities were looking for me to deport me. A pastor named W. H. Hampton knew about my situation and wrote a letter to a school in St. Louis on my behalf. When the school accepted me and sent the information to the immigration authorities, I regained my status as a student. But that meant I was leaving California and the girl I was falling in love with.

I DECIDED TO BELIEVE GOD FOR GREAT
THINGS, JUST AS SISTER AIMEE HAD DONE.

"Donna," I said as the time approached, "I don't want to go to St. Louis without you."

I had put her on the spot, as uncomfortable as it was. I didn't want to go through life without her.

"Would you marry me?" I asked. She had almost no time to make a decision. I was leaving in a matter of days. After a moment she turned to me.

"Yes, Elias," she said, and broke into the most beautiful smile I had ever seen. We hugged, and I felt almost as happy as I did when I met the Lord.

We had no time for a proper wedding, so we eloped in Yuma, Arizona. A Pentecostal preacher married us on September 17, 1953. I did not know then that if I had married without having legal status it would have created a whole host of problems for me. But God was fulfilling the scripture He had given me on the boat. Even when I didn't know all the laws, He moved ahead to protect me.

Three days later, my bride and I bundled everything we had in my Studebaker and drove to St. Louis, which for me was like going to another country. Donna had eighty dollars to her name; I had thirty-four and the car. We arrived at 2300 Miami Street where we rented a room on the fourth floor. Donna got an office job, and I worked for Beeble Brothers roofing company during the day—the hardest physical labor I had ever engaged in. As I swung hammers and hefted stacks of shingles onto the roof, I thought back to my job as a contractor in Beirut. Then, laborers had worked for me. Now I was in the opposite position. By the end of each day, every muscle from the smallest to largest ached, and it was all I could do to focus my mind on my schoolwork.

Donna and I both attended Bible school at night. I had given up authority and money in Lebanon to work with Dr. Colby in the church, and ultimately, to come to America to prepare for the ministry. But here I was, breaking my back and living like a starving student. *Was this what ministry training was like?* I wondered. *Do I prepare for ministry by pounding nails all day in the hot sun, then sitting in a classroom at night, trying to learn Greek and Hebrew while forcing my eyelids to defy gravity?* My pain eased a little when I was promoted to truck driver for the crew, pulling an asphalt kettle from job to job. But each day was like a triathlon.

We weren't in St. Louis long. Soon the cold weather came, only adding to the general misery of our situation. I was still working for the roofing company, and now the snow made every task much more difficult. Even our apartment offered only limited comfort at the end of the day, as we had to share a bathroom with other tenants. Fed up, we finally decided to try for a better situation elsewhere. I enrolled at Life Bible College in Los Angeles, the school founded by the great evangelist Aimee Semple McPherson, and by the time we moved back to that deliciously warmer climate, Donna was expecting our first child. We settled into a dormitory room for married couples. Our room boasted a hideaway bed and a small kitchen, but we still had to share the bathroom with another student. I can't imagine he enjoyed sharing a bathroom with a pregnant woman.

Los Angeles was much more to our liking. I got a job as the school janitor, working every afternoon scrubbing windows and bathrooms and keeping the alleys outside the 5,500-seat Angelus Temple auditorium clean. I considered it an honor to serve in such a grand, historic place. I thought back to the days when Sister Aimee preached, drawing thousands of people to her meetings via trolley cars from all over Los Angeles. She fed millions, encouraged countless people by radio, and started a denomination that took the full gospel to every continent on earth.

She was a person of big vision, and as I swept the aisles of the church she had built, I let my own vision soar. I didn't want to settle for anything less than the biggest, best plan that God had for my ministry in the Middle East. Angelus Temple was a monument to the fact that with God, all things were possible to him who believed (Mark 10:27). As I cleaned the windows and gathered trash in the alleyways, over and over again I decided to believe God for great things, just as Sister Aimee had done.

But on the practical side, Donna and I had to fight for basic survival. Our finances were like the punch line of a joke. I made fifty dollars a week—exactly the cost of our rent. Our car payment was another fifty dollars a month, leaving us with one hundred dollars left over to pay for my tuition, schoolbooks, food, and living expenses. Donna sometimes earned a little extra money by babysitting for other couples who attended the college, but still there was not enough money to cover everything we needed.

The temptation to quit school and work full time taunted me like an invisible houseguest. I felt angry and humiliated at times because I wasn't providing for my family the way I wanted to. As I swept and mopped Angelus Temple and then came home to write term papers, I also wrestled with bigger questions: Was it really worth it to stay in school? Was this God's plan for my life, or had I chosen a path which made it difficult on us for no good reason? *Perhaps*, I thought, *God would bless my ministry without Bible school training.*

But God protected me from my own frustrations and did not allow me to quit school. Instead, He built my faith through the lean times so that one day I would be ready to stand strong and take the gospel to the Middle East in a way nobody had done before. The lessons were hard at the time, but they proved as valuable as gold.

Chapter 5

LEARNING TO LIVE BY FAITH

I N AUGUST 1954, our daughter, Rebecca, was born, and the doctors promptly told Donna and me not to have any more children.

"Your blood types don't match," the doctor told us. "Your children will need blood transfusions when they are born."

But contrary to their expectations, Rebecca had been born healthy, strong, and beautiful, making us a threesome. Even though the lack of adequate income and money continued to drain Donna and me, we kept reminding each other of God's promises. Our faith was becoming more resilient and rooted. We were learning to take each step trusting in God alone, not in our circumstances or what our eyes could see.

The Lord opened doors for me to preach and receive offerings during the first few months after Rebecca was born. Then, when our first Christmas as parents rolled around, most churches shut their doors to visiting speakers. In spite of our upbeat mood, we were almost penniless.

Christmas Eve came, and that morning Donna stirred up a small bowl of gravy for our breakfast. It was the last item in our pantry. Donna fed Becky a special formula that was necessary because she had allergies.

"I have one dollar left in my pocket," I told Donna matter-of-factly. "We can go to your parents' house tonight and probably have enough gas in the car to make it home. But let's not go on Christmas Day, because they exchange gifts then, and I don't want them to know how badly in need we are. We can't even afford to buy them anything."

I WAS LOOKING FORWARD TO SEEING HOW HE PROVIDED A MIRACLE.

We fasted that day, and that night we went to her parents' house for a joyful occasion. Though we were down to our last dollar, we had seen God care for us before, and I knew He would not let us down. I had grown strong at fighting the battle of faith in my mind during adverse circumstances.

"Elias," Donna's father said as we visited, "would you mind taking me to the drug store? I have to buy one more present for a friend."

I agreed, knowing it would use even more of our precious

gas. While we were at the store, a little doll on the shelf caught my eye. It was small and not well made, but I picked it up anyway. I couldn't resist using my last dollar to buy it for Becky. I couldn't let her first Christmas go by without getting her a gift. I took it to the register and set my last dollar on the counter.

"Merry Christmas," said the clerk, putting the doll into a bag and handing me a receipt.

"Merry Christmas," I replied, and it was like a small declaration of faith.

When we got back to Donna's parents' house, I took Donna aside and whispered that I had used the dollar to buy Becky a doll. We were officially broke.

The evening was restful and pleasant, but in the back of my mind I could picture us running out of gas on the way home—a man, his wife, and their new baby daughter stranded on Christmas Eve. I could see myself pushing the car down empty streets, trying to find an open gas station. But I knew that God would not let me be put to shame if I trusted in Him, as David had written in Psalm 25:3. God would make a way, even if we ran out of gas. In a way, I was looking forward to seeing how He provided a miracle.

We left the house and said our good-byes. The test was about to begin. Every block we drove felt like it went on forever; every noise the car made sounded like the engine was stalling. One mile went by, and another. The gas seemed to be holding, and I was thankful, even cheerful.

"Help us, Lord," Donna prayed audibly, holding Becky in her arms. Like me, she was learning to trust the Lord in all situations. God was building us both up in preparation for the difficult work we would encounter in the Middle East.

After what seemed like an eternity, we finally arrived at a point only several blocks away from Angelus Temple where we lived. At the top of the hill on Sunset Boulevard, the engine sputtered and stalled. I turned the key, and the engine made an awful noise. The tank was dry, but we were on a hill, and our apartment was at the bottom. With the engine off we began to coast down, down, down, picking up speed.

"Make it, make it," I coaxed, feeling as if angels were pulling us home. Everything sounded so quiet in the absence of the running engine. Becky cooed, unaware of our plight. We passed the houses along the block as our car coasted over the pavement. Quiet as a church mouse, the car was like a shadow slipping through the night.

The car slowed as we neared the bottom of the hill. Gently, I steered it into our parking space in front of the dorm. With just enough momentum, the car came to a stop in the space. I stepped on the brake, put it into parking gear, and looked over at Donna. She was looking at me. We laughed and sighed with relief, thanking God for His Christmas Eve gift of getting us home.

But another surprise awaited us when we stepped into the dorm room. As I turned on the light, Donna pointed to the kitchen table and said, "Elias, look!" There was an oversized box of groceries—chicken, dressing, potatoes, cranberry sauce, and everything else we needed for a Christmas dinner. It even contained Becky's special formula, which no one knew about except Donna's family.

We looked at each other, wide-eyed, wondering who

could have brought it. "Our dorm mother," I said. Donna nodded.

Within a minute we were down knocking on the door of our dormitory mother's apartment to thank her for the food. She opened the door, and Donna embraced her. "Thank you so much for the food," Donna said. "I don't know how you knew we were low on money, but it was so thoughtful of you."

⌒

WITH EVERY CHALLENGE, HE WAS SHOWING US THAT WE MUST RELY ON THE PROVISION THAT CAME FROM HIS HAND.

⌒

"Yes, thank you so much," I offered.

The dorm mother appeared perplexed by our gratitude.

"I didn't get you anything," she said. "I didn't even know you were low on money."

Donna looked at me. "But somebody put a box of groceries on our table," she said. "I know the door was locked. I always check it before we leave the house."

"Nobody went in there," our dorm mother said. "I have the only other key, and I didn't let anyone in."

We stood in silence for a moment. Then our dorm mother came out with us.

"I insist on seeing this box of food," she said, and we went upstairs together to our apartment. We all looked at the box as if it were a strange machine none of us understood.

Then I pulled a few things from it to show her the bounty it contained.

"Honestly, kids," she said, staring at the stacks of food and shaking her head. "I didn't let anyone in. It must have been an angel."

That box of food lasted us two weeks until I preached again. It also boosted my faith even further. Not long after that, on a Sunday morning, I woke up knowing that our car payment was due, and I hated to be late. I was praying about this when suddenly I felt that God had given us an answer. I got off my knees and went to the door.

"Where are you going?" Donna said as I passed by.

"To get my check," I said, and walked out the door, leaving her with a confused expression on her face.

On my way to the mailbox I passed the dorm mother.

"Hello, Elias. Where are you going?" she said.

"To get my check," I said.

"But why?" she said. "This is Sunday. There's no mail on Sunday."

"Yes, I have a check in the mail," I said. I knew full well that we had already checked Saturday's mail. She followed me to the mailbox out of curiosity. I opened it, reached in, and pulled out a registered letter. No one had signed for it. There was no return address on it. In it was a check for exactly enough money to pay our car payment. She was astonished; so was Donna. But I knew we would have to believe for many miracles if we were to survive on the mission field in the Middle East. God was proving that time and again. With every challenge, He was showing us that we must rely on the provision that came from His hand.

God continued to have mercy on us, and soon brought a huge financial opportunity right to our door. One afternoon I came home from school for lunch, and as I got ready to go to work at Angelus Temple, I heard a knock on the door. A man was standing there with a big grin on his face and a stack of items under his arm.

"Hello," he said. "My name is Doug Teeble. May I come in? I have something to show you."

I invited him in.

"I have the King James version of the New Testament on record albums," he said. "I also have wonderful Christian music by different artists."

FOR ONCE, OUR BANK ACCOUNT WAS OVERFLOWING, AND DONNA AND I BASKED IN THE GOODNESS OF GOD.

He spread out a collection of records by artists such as George Beverly Shea, Ralph Carmichael, the Spencer family, Stuart Hamblin, and many others. The records looked like diamonds to me, laying there on the coffee table. In those days there was no Christian television and only a few Christian programs on the radio. I was starved for good Christian music.

"How much do the records cost?" I asked.

"It's $64.95 for the set," he said. "That includes a small

record player. You can buy it in installments, if you like."

I only had five dollars to spare. But I didn't really even have that much because a week earlier the dean of the college, Dr. Clarence Hall, had called me into his office to tell me that I owed seven hundred dollars for my tuition.

"Elias, graduation is in three months," he had said. "You cannot graduate unless you pay your bill."

But sitting there with Doug in my living room, I had an inspired idea. Perhaps I could sell records to raise money to pay my tuition.

"Can I sell these records like you do?" I asked.

"Sure," he said. "But you have to buy the demo."

"I can't afford it," I said, thinking of the milk I had to buy for Becky. "But I still would like to sell them."

"Tell you what," he said. "Let's make an appointment, and I'll introduce you to my boss, Earl Williams. He's the founder and owner of Sacred Records, which, as I told you, is the first and only Christian record company of its time. Mr. Williams was the song leader for Aimee Simple McPherson many years ago."

We shook hands, and Doug went back to his sales route. A few days later I met with him and Earl Williams. Mr. Williams was cordial to me as I explained my situation to him, and he heard me out. He was quiet for a moment, then turned to Doug.

"Give him the demo set, and teach him how to write the contracts and sell the product," he said.

Doug gave me the demo set and showed me how to write the contracts and present the product. That was all I needed. Earl Williams had seen something in me that spurred him to take a chance, and I didn't intend to let him down. I spoke about the records with everybody I saw. I made appointments with people to do demonstrations in their homes, and God was with me. By the end of the first week, I had sold more records than any other salesman in the company for that week. I was able to quit my job as the school janitor. The first month I made so much money that I won a gold watch worth a hundred dollars. It seemed that wherever I went, I made a sale.

Leads kept pouring in. Earl Williams advertised on the radio and invited people to receive a demonstration of the product in their home. He divided the leads among his sales team. If I went somewhere to do a demo, and the people were not saved, I told them about Jesus, prayed with them, and sold them the records. When another salesman could not make a sale, they sent me to do the job, and 99 percent of the time I succeeded where they had failed. Soon people in the company had a saying: "If Malki can't make the sale, nobody can. It will never be sold."

Finally, Dr. Hall, the dean of the college, called me into his office.

"What are you doing to our students?" he said. "They are all going into debt to buy your records."

"I want to graduate," I told him. "You told me I have to pay seven hundred dollars in tuition."

There was nothing he could say to that. I was being industrious, and the people who bought the records were getting the finest Christian music available. A week before graduation I took seven hundred dollars in cash and paid my outstanding tuition bill. I also had enough to pay off my car. For once, our bank account was overflowing, and Donna and I basked in the goodness of God.

But even with the success, my heart yearned for the Middle East. I wanted to serve the Lord back in Lebanon, but I knew I needed more experience in the ministry. I was simply too green to return to the Middle East so soon. I graduated from Life Bible College in June 1955 with a class of one hundred sixteen. We called our class the "Messengers of Hope." Right after graduation I took a job pioneering a church in the city of Highland near San Bernardino.

When I told Mr. Williams I was quitting as a salesman for Sacred Records, he almost cried. "You can still sell the records, Elias," he said.

"I'm sorry, Mr. Williams," I said. "It's time for me to work full time for the Lord."

~ॐ Chapter 6 ॐ~

HEALED AND RECOMMISSIONED

THE STOREFRONT BUILDING in Highland, California, where I would pastor my first church didn't resemble a thriving church; it was more like a broken-down shack—but I saw great potential there. The former pastor had closed the church six months earlier, and the grass and weeds in front of the building were nearly four feet high. The inside of the building was a mess. There were no members except for one elderly lady, Sister Harmon, who kept the church's books. We were starting from scratch, but I knew God would do a great work if we continued to follow the path He laid out.

Donna and I rented a small apartment to live in, and the church district gave us two hundred dollars a month. We were happy to supplement that with the money I had made from the sales of records. Donna and I, along with Sister Harmon, put our muscles into repairing the facility. Before long, God sent people to help us. Within months we held a water baptism service and baptized seven people, among them Donna's sister and brother-in-law who had been saved in our church. Steadily more people came and were saved, and I was overjoyed at our early success. To make life even sweeter, in May of the following year our second daughter, Ruth, was born.

Like any new pastor, I had taken the church in Highland dreaming of what it could become. I poured myself into making it grow, reaching out to the community and putting together a team to do great exploits for the Lord. Donna and I were thrilled to be working under the blessing of the Lord. But in all our confidence, I did not recognize the enemy's efforts to bring the church down through people we counted as friends. It was one of the most difficult and painful lessons I had yet learned, but one that made us wiser and stronger than ever.

I put a certain gentleman and his wife in charge of our adult Sunday school class, but I was naïve and did not see that they were undermining my authority, just as King David's son Absalom had undermined him in the Bible account. When I finally confronted this man about it, he quit and persuaded half of the people to leave with him. For a church of thirty to forty people this was devastating, and I took the defeat hard. Our Sunday morning attendance shrunk back to a dozen or so. All the work we had engaged in for a year was walking out the door because of a rebellious layman, and I could do nothing but pray and watch the people go.

This was not what we had been told to expect in Bible college. I became consumed with getting the church back on solid ground, and I felt as if the entire burden had fallen on me to turn the mess the devil had made into a miracle. Soon my body showed signs of the strain I had placed myself under. I began to have stomach cramps. We had no medical insurance, so we only went to the doctor in times of emergency. I tried to treat myself as best I could, but that June the situation got beyond me. I took Donna and our two daughters to Big Bear, where Donna and I had first met, to celebrate Donna's birthday. I loved water and swimming, having been raised by the shores of the Mediterranean Sea, and so we rented a boat and went on the lake. But soon I felt weak and tired.

DONNA AND I WERE THRILLED TO BE WORKING UNDER THE BLESSING OF THE LORD. BUT IN ALL OUR CONFIDENCE, I DID NOT RECOGNIZE THE ENEMY'S EFFORTS.

"Are you OK?" Donna asked, looking at me with concern.

"I'm fine," I said.

She waited a moment before commenting, "You don't look so good. Maybe we had better go back to shore."

I didn't resist but rowed the boat back, got into the car, and drove us home from our disappointing outing.

"I'm sorry. I let you and the kids down," I said as we wound down the mountain.

"It's OK, Elias," she said, rubbing my arm, but I still felt bad for her.

"You have such a full schedule raising the children, and with the church going the way it has been going, I wanted to give you a break from it all," I said. "It's your birthday."

"I had a good time," she said. "I'm more worried about you."

"I'll be all right," I said, though my stomach didn't feel all right.

I was supposed to preach the next morning, a Sunday, but my stomach was in constant pain. For two weeks I had been passing dark stool. Donna thought it was due to my iron levels, but time would reveal it was much worse than that. That night I took two aspirin and went to bed, and when I woke up in the night to use the bathroom, I vomited blood. Donna gasped when she saw it.

"Elias!"

She ran to the telephone and called our neighbor. I lay there waiting for him, and he put me in his car and took me to Loma Linda Hospital. There I vomited blood again, and they took me into the emergency room and started me on a blood transfusion. My condition had gone beyond what I could control.

I did not sleep that night. Doctors put a tube down my nose to pump the blood from my stomach and to keep me from vomiting. I had blood going into one arm and an intravenous tube in the other, but it wasn't doing me any good. A stomach ulcer was putting out more blood than the transfusion was putting into me.

"He is bleeding faster than we can replace the blood," the doctor told Donna. "He is so weak and anemic that we can't perform surgery to remove the ulcer. He would die if we operated on him."

"What do we do?" she asked.

"We'll have to wait and see if he gets strong enough for us to operate," he said.

Three nights passed, and soon they removed the man who was sharing my room. I knew I was getting worse. I had difficulty breathing, though I never lost consciousness. My doctor called Donna at midnight.

"I don't think your husband will live through the night," he said. "We have done everything we can. You should call your relatives and friends to come and see him."

I didn't hear him say this, but about that time I started talking to the Lord because I sensed I would not make it.

GOD HAD SPARED MY LIFE AND RECOMMISSIONED ME FOR THE WORK FOR WHICH I HAD BEEN BORN.

"Lord, how come I am dying now?" I said. "You said You were going to use me in the Middle East to preach the gospel. You brought me to this country to finish my education. All my work here has been about preparing for the day I would return home and fulfill the destiny You gave me when I was young."

I thought of my grandfather and father and the sacrifices

they had made to stand for Christ in hostile territory. I had patterned my life after their example, and I desperately wanted to do even more, with God's help. Then the voice of the Lord answered me.

"Do you want to go back to the Middle East, or do you want to come to Me?" He said.

"Lord, I want to go to the Middle East," I said, then added, "but the organization will not send me."

"I will send you," He said. "Will you go?"

"Yes, Lord, I will go."

Just then I heard with my natural ears the nurse arguing with someone in the hallway. Donna had called her former pastor, Faye Spencer, and asked him to come and pray for me. Faye arrived at the hospital at 1:00 a.m., not long after my conversation with the Lord, and I heard him arguing with the nurse in the hallway.

"I must go in there!" he said.

"Sir, you may not," she said. "Visiting hours are over."

"I was called here by the family," he said. "I'm a minister."

"I'm sorry, I can't let you in," she insisted.

I yelled as loud as I could, "Let him in!"

A moment later, Faye came into my hospital room and laid his hand on me. He said only one sentence: "Brother Elias, in the name of Jesus be made whole. Good night."

He walked out of the room, and I fell into a deep sleep.

At noon the next day, I woke up free of the IV and the tubes that had been in my nose. My doctor walked into my room and said, "Reverend, it is a miracle that you are alive."

"Yes," I said. "The Lord healed me."

He was a Christian man, and he agreed with me.

I wanted to go home immediately, but he insisted I stay for four days for observation. Four days later I was released, weighing six pounds more than when I was admitted. God had spared my life and recommissioned me for the work for which I had been born. I was honored and humbled by His grace to me, and I felt more certain than ever that soon we would leave the United States for the mission field.

It took me two weeks to gain my strength back. And because we lacked insurance, I had a substantial medical bill to pay. I took a job in a grocery store, stocking shelves from 1:00 a.m. to 10:00 a.m., five days a week. I slept when I could and continued to pastor the church.

A year later, the enemy took another shot at our family. Donna was about to give birth to our third child. We were adding two rooms to the house, and we had turned off the electricity so Donna's father and brother could work on the wiring. Our daughter Ruth, a little over a year old, was playing quietly in the room with Donna, but Donna didn't know that her father had turned the electricity back on. She was busy working when she looked over and saw Ruth's body shaking unnaturally. Our precious baby had thrust two nails in the electrical socket and was being electrocuted.

Donna bolted toward her, tripped over a sawhorse and tumbled down. As she hit the ground, she kicked Ruth away from the socket. Ruth survived unharmed, but the fall hurt Donna, and she was concerned about the baby inside her. She called the doctor.

"The baby is already in the birth canal," he said. "If you are not in pain at this moment, just take it easy. Everything will be fine."

But his advice sat uneasily with her. That night while we were sleeping, Donna woke up and heard someone come in our bedroom door. Because of the remodeling, our bed was in a narrow room with the girls' cribs next to us. As she reached up to turn on the light, she saw a man standing at the foot of our bed. He didn't speak at first.

"Who are you?" Donna said. "How did you get in here?"

"That's not important," he said. "Do you really think I am letting you get away from me? You turned your back on me, and I am going to kill your son."

"No, you're not," she said.

"Yes," he said. She noticed he had evil eyes.

"You are not going to kill my son. You leave him alone," she said. He hissed at her, and Donna started screaming.

"Oh yes," he said again. "I am going to kill your son."

I woke up with Donna's shrieks in my ears.

"What's wrong?" I said.

"There's a man in here telling me he is going to kill my son."

I reached up and turned the light on. There was no one there.

Donna was deeply affected by the event, and she prayed much in the next few days. Weeks passed, and five days before the baby was born, she dreamed she was giving birth. She saw herself lying on the delivery table, and she asked the doctor if the baby was a boy or girl. "It's a boy, and he is perfect," the doctor said in the dream. Donna saw the baby's red hair and light blue eyes. Then she woke up.

The next morning she told me, "Our baby is going to be OK, and it's a boy."

I shook my head.

"No. Everyone says you are carrying it like a girl," I said, but she was convinced otherwise.

<hr>

THE LORD SPOKE TO ME THAT IT WAS TIME TO RETURN TO LEBANON.

<hr>

Five days later she entered a very difficult labor. They gave her as much anesthesia as they could, then had to stop so not to affect the baby. They gave her laughing gas instead, and she laughed through much of the labor. The baby was indeed a boy, but when Donna had fallen a few weeks earlier, he was pulled up out of the birth canal feet first. His head was now stuck in her pelvic girdle, and they couldn't get him out. Other doctors rushed in to help. They broke her pelvic girdle to dislodge him. When our son was finally born, the doctor held him, but he didn't cry.

"What's wrong?" Donna said.

"I don't know," the doctor said, inspecting the baby with great urgency. Then after a while he stopped. His shoulders sagged.

"I'm sorry Donna," he said. "We couldn't save him."

The nurse who had been waiting for the baby wheeled the empty incubator out of the room. The doctor held our son's body. It was completely still. Donna saw the baby's red hair, and remembering her dream she prayed, "Lord, you told me my baby was going to live."

"Waahh!"

The room was filled with the baby's first cry. The doctor

watched as the child's body turned pink.

"Nurse!" he said, surprised to the point of alarm. The nurse with the incubator brought it back into the room and tended to the newborn. Other doctors bandaged Donna from knees to chest. She couldn't walk or go to the other room to see our son, whom we named Timothy.

Our baby was not out of the woods. He was having difficulty breathing and swallowing, and I prayed throughout those critical hours. The next morning the doctor came in smiling and said, "Donna, do you want to see your baby? He just drank a bottle of milk. I don't think he is having trouble swallowing anymore." They brought him in and Donna held him, but when he opened his eyes, she was anxious—Donna is part American Indian, and in her culture, light blue eyes mean a person is blind. She called quickly for the doctor and exclaimed, "Doctor, he's blind!"

"No, he's fine," said the doctor. "We examined him." Then Donna remembered the Lord had told her he would have light blue eyes, and for the first time mother and son cuddled together in peace.

With barely a pause, the Lord spoke to me that it was time to return to Lebanon, but we needed money. The organization we belonged to would not send us because Lebanon was too dangerous a place to start missionary work. But I resigned the Highland church in obedience to the Lord and went to my good friend Earl Williams and started working for Sacred Records again. He was glad to have me back and made me district manager in northern California. Donna and I found a house in San Jose, the nicest one we had lived in yet, with two bathrooms, a dining room, and a back yard, all luxuries to us. I sold records during the week and preached every weekend as an evangelist. God gave me great favor, and I made more money than I ever had—two thousand dollars a month. I bought my first brand-new car and recruited twelve people to work for me. They bought demo sets from me, and I made commission on everything they sold. We produced more sales than any other district.

But my thoughts were inescapably in Lebanon.

I applied for American citizenship and for my passport. We saved twelve thousand dollars in one year. But during that time I wasn't sure if Donna agreed with me about our calling to the Middle East. I wondered if she would prefer that we stay in San Jose, especially since we were so financially blessed. As Christmas 1958 approached, she came to me one day, embraced me, and said, "Let's make this the best Christmas we've ever had."

"Why do you say that?" I asked, looking at her beautiful face.

"You know why," she said. "Because you are going to Lebanon, and I am going with you."

I was speechless. I held her close, and in my heart I said, *Thank You, Jesus, for speaking to both of us.*

With hearts united, we printed prayer cards with our family's picture on them, distributed them to our friends, and announced that we were leaving for the mission field. I obtained American citizenship and received a passport. Then I asked the Lord for a final sign that we were doing the right thing: I wanted one person to buy all of our furniture.

One day there was a knock at my door.

"I am Pastor Leroy Wright," the man said, "and I am looking for a place to rent."

"This place is for rent, and all the furniture you see is for sale for a thousand dollars," I said. "Are you interested?"

"Yes," he said. "I will take the house and the furniture."

With that confirmation in mind, we bought a trailer to live in during the few months before we left. I sold our car. People heard about our decision to go to the mission field and began to send offerings. A woman named Ruth in San Fernando called us and said the Lord woke her up at night and told her to send us seven hundred dollars, the biggest offering we had ever received.

Three months later we sold our trailer for a five-hundred-dollar profit, bought large packing trunks, and filled them with our possessions. We drove from California to New York, where my American journey had begun. In a fitting coda, we boarded a steamship for South Hampton, England, then took a plane from London to Beirut, arriving in the Middle East in September 1959. I felt like I had never left.

My seven years in the United States had transformed my life and given me a family, training, and ministry experience. I had left Beirut a naïve baby Christian. I was returning with a little more wisdom and an even greater commitment to the vision of reaching the Middle East. Now it was time to rejoin the battle on the frontlines. It wouldn't take long for us to learn we were in hostile territory. But we knew God had gone ahead of us and would keep us safe and give us a fruitful ministry.

With faith welling up in our hearts, we had finally arrived in the Middle East—the mission field God had called me to as a boy.

Solomon Malki, uncle of Elias, who was martyred by Kurdish Muslims who invaded his village in Karadesh, Turkey, during the Turkish Holy War just after World War I. John Malki, Elias's grandfather, who had been the first Christian missionary to Karadesh, Turkey, was also beheaded on the same day.

Presbyterian church in Kurdistan, Turkey, where Elias's grandfather, John, was saved. Forty-six years after the massacre, Elias preached in this church in 1964.

Elias, in 1944 at age thirteen at St. Luke's, the Anglican mission school where he attended grade school in Haifa.

Elias (wearing hat) in Beirut, Lebanon, in January 1951 shortly after he was saved.

Elias Malki with his mother and father and siblings in 1952. Back row, left to right: Zeny, John, Elias, Mary, Rebecca. Front row, left to right: Paul, Sarah, Aziz (father), Peter, Salimi (mother), and Rashael. Not pictured: Solomon (deceased earlier) and David.

Dr. Flora Colby, the missionary speaker who preached the night in January 1951 when Elias gave his heart to the Lord.

Elias was youth leader for this group of young people at Dr. Flora Colby's mission in 1951.

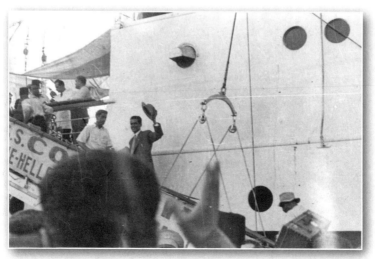

Taken October 6, 1952, when Elias left Lebanon to go to America to attend Bible School.

Elias Malki as a young preacher in 1953.

Elias with his mother, father, and brothers John and Paul
on October 6, 1952, the day he left for America.

Elias Malki in 1955 at his graduation from Life Bible College in Los Angeles, California.

Elias and his bride, Donna, pictured in a park in Illinois shortly after they married in October 1953.

Elias, Donna, and their first daughter, Becky, in
November 1955.

Taken in 1956 at the Loma Linda Hospital in
Highland, California where Elias was treated
for a stomach ulcer that was miraculously healed
by God.

Elias Malki in 1962 at thirty-one
years of age.

A picture of the congregation in the church Elias pastored in Beirut,
Lebanon, in the early 1960s.

Pastor Malki baptizing someone who was saved
in his church in Beirut.

The Sunday school in Elias's church in Beirut in 1962.

Elias and son Timothy on board the SS *Constitution* during their return trip to Beirut after furlough in America in 1962.

Dr. Elias Malki with his family in 1965. Pictured left to right: Timothy, Daniel, Elias, Rebecca, Donna, and Ruth.

Elias and Donna Malki in November 1965.

Campers at the Charismatic summer camp in Lebanon that Elias
opened in 1970 for people from Syria, Lebanon, Jordan, and Egypt.

War in Lebanon. Pictured in Beirut in late 1975.

Elias Malki with some of the campers attending the Charismatic
summer camp in Lebanon in 1970.

Raffoul Najem (in cap and gown) and Gebrael Mourad,
students at Bible college in Beirut, Lebanon.

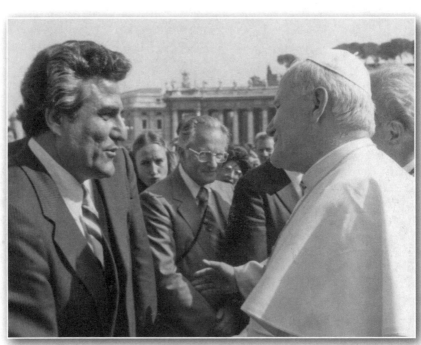

Dr. Malki with Pope John Paul II in 1978 during the eight-day
dialogue at the Vatican between Pentecostal and Catholic leaders.
Dr. Malki represented the Middle East.

Dr. Elias Malki and his daughter Rebecca (co-host) on the set of the
Good News program in 1983.

Mego Christian Center, opened in Cyprus by Elias in 1993 as a
training center for new Arab Christians.

Elias Malki and the archbishop of Cyprus, 1995.

Elias pictured at the satellite uplink in London, England, for his
Good News Program, 1996. Dr. Malki was the first man in the Christian
community ministering to Arabs via satellite.

Elias Malki with the president of Cyprus in 1999.

Dr. Malki with Yasser Arafat in 1995.

Elias Malki with Yasser Arafat in 1994.

Elias Malki with Yasser Arafat in 1996 when he presented Arafat with a treasured gold coin that was the only one missing from Arafat's collection.

~ↄ   Chapter 7   ↄ~

TO THE
MIDDLE EAST—WITH
GOD'S POWER

B ACK IN LEBANON I checked up on old friends and caught
up on the news, both happy and sad. Dr. Colby was
no longer in Lebanon, and other missionaries had
taken her place. Nicholas, who I learned had spread the gossip about me seven years earlier, had immigrated to Brazil
and become a successful car dealer. Then one day a man
walked into his office and shot him to death. It was grievous
news. Even though Nicholas had caused me trouble, I had
never wished him harm.

I was overjoyed to see my father, mother, brothers, and
sisters. Some members of my family were already following the path I had blazed to America. Two brothers and

one sister had moved there, and Mom and Dad spoke seriously of it.

"There is no opportunity for poor people in Lebanon," they told me time and again as we shared a meal and watched the children play. "You are born either rich or poor, and there isn't much you can do to change it."

I helped my parents get visas to go to the United States. Mom left first, then Dad, and Donna and I wished them as many blessings in the States as we had experienced there. I became the guardian of my younger brothers and sisters—a tough job, but one God helped me with. Eventually, all my siblings moved to the United States, and I was left alone in Lebanon with my wife and children. Our reunion with my side of the family had been rich, but short-lived.

AS I SHARED WITH HIM ABOUT THE GOODNESS OF THE LORD, GOD OPENED THIS MAN'S HEART TO HEAR MY WORDS.

Donna and I got down to the work God had called us to immediately. We started a mission church in a town called Sinelfeel, a suburb of Beirut. Ours was the first evangelical church there, and we met in our house and used the living room for a sanctuary. On Sundays we set out chairs, and when the service ended, we put away the chairs and had our living room again. It was a perfect portrait of how we lived—with ministry and our personal lives intertwined.

My first convert was a former classmate of mine from high

school who had become a politician in a powerful political party. His name was Shaheen. We spotted each other one day on the street and discovered we were neighbors. We had not seen each other in ten years, so I invited him to church, but he could not come. I invited him instead to my home, and he gladly accepted.

We sat on the balcony of our home one evening. The moon was shining. A nice breeze was blowing, and we reminisced about old times. He told me of his victories and disappointments. He was married but could not have children, but he had secured a good position for himself in a political party.

As we talked I sensed the presence and guidance of the Holy Spirit. Throughout the conversation the Lord opened my mouth to speak the right words. As I shared with him about the goodness of the Lord, God opened this man's heart to hear my words. I sensed he was taking in all that the Lord was saying to him. Before the evening was over, we agreed that the next day we would go fishing together. His father was a commercial fisherman, and Shaheen was an expert at throwing the net.

"I love to go fishing," he said, relishing the thought. "Tomorrow, I will teach you how to throw a net."

He was getting ready to leave, but I felt there was unfinished business.

"Shaheen," I said, "I know we only just began to speak about the Lord, but would you like to pray with me to receive Him?"

I knew it would be difficult for him to say yes to Christ and remain a member of the political party he was involved in, but he responded without any hesitation.

"I would like to pray with you," he said.

I held his hand and asked him to repeat the sinner's prayer after me. He did, right there on the balcony of my home. Then he went home.

"Donna," I said as we prepared to turn in, "the Lord worked so quickly in his heart. It was amazing. But I wonder if he has a difficult road ahead."

The next morning I picked up Shaheen from his home, only about two blocks from mine. We drove toward the beautiful Mediterranean beach. I saw many places and sights along the way that I had not seen in years. For me it was a special homecoming. At the sea, we spent a few hours talking, and he taught me how to throw a net. Then we went back to our neighborhood, and I dropped him off at his home. He waved, and I waved back. Then I drove home and parked the car at my house. I had barely gone inside and sat down when we heard machine gun shots ring out from the direction of Shaheen's home.

"What was that?" Donna said. I jumped out of my chair and ran out of the house and down the street to where Shaheen lived. There he lay in the street in a widening pool of his own blood. He was dead. His political enemies had murdered him in front of his house.

I felt frozen in time. The very hands he had used to teach me to throw a net into the sea now lay lifeless at his side. People began to arrive and look on the body of this man with whom I had shared such rich and nuanced conversation the night before.

Why did this happen? I asked myself. *Why did they shoot him? Why now?* I had no answer. The next afternoon was his funeral, and I did what I could to comfort the family. The following day I went to visit them again. Shaheen's father and I sat alone for a while. His hands were the knotty, coarse hands of a fisherman—an expert net thrower. I thought of the nets Shaheen and I had thrown into the sea two days earlier. I thought about how unfair it was for a man to have to attend his son's funeral.

THOUGH I DIDN'T UNDERSTAND WHY SHAHEEN HAD DIED IN THE MANNER AND PLACE IN WHICH HE DID, I KNEW GOD WAS CONFIRMING SOMETHING IN THE TRAGIC CIRCUMSTANCE.

Shaheen's father shifted quietly in his seat, as if perched on an uncomfortable cushion. Then, after he could take no more, he leaned over to me.

"There is something I must tell you," he said, looking around to see that nobody else was near. "The other night when my son came home from your house, I could not believe my ears. I thought Shaheen would never say such a thing. He reached into his pocket and took out the badge that he wore on his lapel, which represented his political party. He handed it to me and said, 'Dad, I don't want to belong to this party anymore. I cannot and serve Jesus Christ. Here—take this badge. I prayed with Elias tonight and accepted Jesus into my life.'"

I felt a rush of peace flood over me as Shaheen's father spoke. God had brought Shaheen and I together the night before his death, and God had intervened to rescue his soul from the enemy. Though I didn't understand why Shaheen had died in the manner and place in which he did, I knew God was confirming something in the tragic circumstance: He wanted Donna and me back in Lebanon, and our work there would help snatch many more people from the jaws of hell.

The church we had started began to grow. As we began holding meetings three times a week, God saved a group of young men, and they brought their friends to hear the gospel. We were on the verge of growing rapidly in a short amount of time. But one day during that time, I had to rush Donna to the hospital. It was six months before the birth of our son, Daniel, and the doctor had warned us it would be dangerous to have the baby.

"There is a 99 percent chance that this baby will require a blood transfusion right away when it is born," he said, referring to the problem Donna and I had because of our Rh blood factor incompatibility. I had heard that before. Each time we had a child, the doctors came to us with their concerned looks and anxious prognoses. And each time they were wrong.

"Then I'll believe God for that 1 percent chance," I said.

The Lord honored my faith, and Daniel was born completely healthy. He did not need a blood transfusion.

But when he was five months old, an epidemic of dehydration swept through Lebanon, and many children died. Daniel got sick and was in the hospital for days. When it appeared he had recovered, we took him home, but he suddenly lapsed into a coma. We rushed him back to the hospital, and they put an IV into his little arm, but the feed didn't work well, and the fluid backed up into his arms and legs. His veins started collapsing. The situation was critical, but we didn't know how critical.

We went home briefly to check on the rest of the kids, and as I was praying, I suddenly jumped up and said, "No, I am not going to believe that."

"Elias, what's happening?" Donna said.

"No, I am not going to believe it," I repeated. Something in my spirit knew there was a bad report about Daniel. We didn't have a phone, so I ran down the street to call the doctor. His report was grim, as I had expected. I sprinted back to Donna.

"I GUESS YOUR GOD DID IT," HE SAID AS IF THIS WAS NO BIG DEAL, AND HE LEFT THE ROOM.

"The doctor said if we want to see our son alive we had better get down there quickly," I said.

We rushed back to the hospital and walked in to see Daniel with his arms and legs swollen like balloons. He was covered in ice packs. I barely recognized my precious little boy. Donna and I prayed for him right then, and then I ran down the hall to see the doctor.

"Elias, there is nothing else I can do for him," the doctor said sadly.

"You have to do something," I pressed.

One of the doctors, a Muslim, looked on skeptically. "There is nothing your God can do now," he said.

"I don't believe that," I retorted.

"There is one more thing we could try," our doctor said. "We could put an IV in his skull."

"Do it!" I said, and ran to the kitchen to get olive oil to anoint Daniel and pray for him. When I got to his room the nurses had shaved Daniel's head of all its black hair in preparation for the IV. As they put the needle in his skull, the swelling went down in his legs, then in his arms. The color returned to his body right up to his hairline. He started crying. It was the most beautiful sound I had heard in years.

"Wow, that worked fast," I said.

"It didn't work at all, Elias," the doctor said. "We haven't put a drop in him yet."

The Muslim doctor, who had come to help and to observe, looked on with veiled surprise.

"I guess your God did it," he said as if this was no big deal, and he left the room.

They kept Daniel in the hospital for a few days, and whenever I visited him, the nurses took me to pray for other people who had the same illness. I even prayed for the doctor's sick daughter. From the day the Lord healed Daniel, no one else in that hospital died of dehydration during the epidemic—including the doctor's daughter.

We continued running the church as best we could with the money we had, but as we followed our convictions it invited conflict with our neighbors. Most people in the area were Catholic or Orthodox, and there were very few Muslims. But one Muslim family lived nearby with their three children in a one-room house. One day the husband and wife got into a quarrel, and both left the house, leaving the children unattended. The children were one year old, three years old, and six months old. They had no food. The Catholic neighbors knew about it but did not report it to the authorities. They left the children there to starve.

When we learned about it, Donna and I went to the house. We found the children half-starved and bitten by rats. We took them in our arms and carried them to our house where Donna cleaned and attended to them. Then we called the authorities who came and took them away. Some people in the neighborhood commended us for stepping in to rescue the children, but others became angry with us. They wished we had left them alone, perhaps to die, for the sake of respecting other peoples' privacy. But we hadn't come to Lebanon to live quietly. We had come to bring the power and love of God to people wherever they were.

By this time, we had been in Lebanon two years. Many young men were getting saved and touched by the Holy Spirit. But our finances kept running out, and I refused to take a secular job. Our money got so low that we needed to come back to America to replenish it, so we rented a building where the church would meet in our absence, and we installed a young man as the pastor.

We used every last penny we had to pay for our tickets to America. The Lord provided a place for us to live in the city of Whittier, California. I immediately contacted my friend Earl Williams at Sacred Records and asked if he could use me. He was happy to hear from me and brought me up to date on the new music package they were selling.

"Go for it, Elias," he said, handing me a demo set. I preached every weekend as an evangelist, and during the week I sold Sacred Records and the Bible on records. God again honored my efforts, and I made enough money to support my family. However, my mind and heart were always in Lebanon with the little flock I had left behind. I felt tender concern for them, even thousands of miles away. I knew my heart would never be settled until I had returned to the Middle East where both my past and my future lay.

THE DOOR WAS WIDE OPEN TO SHARE THE GOSPEL, AND DONNA AND I WERE DETERMINED TO TAKE ADVANTAGE OF IT.

But the money I made working for Sacred Records reminded me how difficult it had been to shoulder such a heavy financial burden for the work in Lebanon.

"Lord," I prayed, "I need to be a part of a missionary organization that will help us raise money to keep going. Otherwise, I don't know how I'll be able to do it."

One night I was listening to the radio, and a friend of mine, Allen Hamilton, preached on the subject, "I will build my church, and the gates of hell will not prevail against it." Hamilton was a former missionary to the Philippines and now was the field representative of the missionary department of the denomination to which I belonged.

"We need laborers to go to the field," he said over the radio, and I began to cry because I was ready to continue my labor, but I didn't have the money. I felt like a shepherd who had abandoned his sheep.

The following Monday morning, I called Hamilton's office.

"You said you needed laborers," I said. "I am ready to go. There is a great need in Lebanon, but we need support. I would like to give you this week to decide if you will support me and my family; otherwise, I am going to seek support somewhere else."

"I will be in touch with you in the next few days," he said, and we prayed together.

On Thursday, I received a call back.

"We have agreed to appoint you as our representative in Lebanon," he said. "We want you to come and meet with us as soon as possible."

With the denomination's support in hand, I carried out my end of the bargain. Donna and I left the children with her mother and drove across the country raising support in churches. Finally, in 1962, we returned to Lebanon. As I stepped back into the warm, dry Mediterranean air with all its familiar smells and sounds, I felt I had slipped back into my own skin. The pain of separation from my flock was over.

In those days the Catholic church controlled Lebanon, and Catholics made up a majority of the population. But evangelical missionaries were given liberty to preach freely under the covering of what we called *the evangelical community*, which was headed up by the Presbyterian church and recognized by the government. I had a good relationship with the head of the Presbyterian committee; he was my former pastor. I operated under his umbrella, and I had the freedom to teach what I wanted to teach. The door was wide open to share the gospel, and Donna and I were determined to take advantage of it.

Soon, we felt called to move to a different district of Beirut. There, we rented a much bigger home than the last one, built homemade benches, set them up in the living room, and began having meetings again. I felt this would be temporary and that God was going to do something much bigger than before. At first the church consisted only of my wife (who was also the piano player), my four children, and myself. Then friends began attending the meetings and learned about being born again and the baptism of the Holy Spirit. One early convert was my brother-in-law, Abraham, who had been addicted to gambling and spent a lot of time at the horse races. He was a successful general contractor in the construction trade, but he squandered his big pay-checks on gambling. The Lord gave me favor with Abraham, and he was saved and baptized in the Holy Spirit. He stopped gambling and became faithful to the church. Some of his brothers and sisters were also touched by the gospel and received the Lord.

Another young man was a communist and atheist, and he had many questions. I spent hours and hours with him in private answering his questions. One night we stayed at the church until 2:00 a.m., and he finally surrendered his life to Christ and became active in the church. He serves the Lord to this day.

A year after we had returned, we were making a bigger impact on Beirut than I had anticipated. I was thrilled to see the gospel going forth in such a difficult, thorny mission field. The church had grown so large that we needed to move to a private villa two blocks from our home. Our weekly schedule was full of prayer meetings, worship services, Sunday school, and youth meetings, and we became well known in the area. Many young people were saved, especially at the Friday night service.

But our work in the Middle East was just beginning, and each day brought new opportunities to prove God's power as we stood in faith against attacks of the enemy.

~ᴄ᙮ Chapter 8 ᙮ᴄ~

Turning Back the Enemy

Satan, our enemy, did not like the fact that God was allowing our work in Lebanon to prosper and win souls into the kingdom of God. Anxious to thwart our plans for evangelism, he sent troublemakers to try to stop our message. These troublemakers launched a loud campaign to interfere with our ministry.

In those days, roads were repaired with tar and asphalt, which were melted in large metal barrels. The city had torn up the street in front of our meeting place and left big chunks of asphalt and empty barrels lying around in the street. The owner of the gambling hall down the street felt that our church was too close to his establishment, so he often sent boys our way to break up our meetings. As we prayed and worshiped, the boys would throw big chunks of asphalt into the barrels, making booming noises that sounded like an army battalion firing its cannons.

One night they did this right before our meeting. The loud *Bam! Bam! Bam!* outside the door drowned out everything—even our thoughts!

"Lord," Donna prayed, "You have stopped many other hindrances, but how are You going to stop this? Elias can't preach over this racket."

"Go outside," the Lord said, and she gladly obeyed, thinking she would yell at the troublemakers and drive them off. But when she got outside, the Lord said, "Look on top of the roof."

THE MORE TROUBLE THE DEVIL CAUSED US, THE MORE THE LORD BLESSED THE WORK.

The roof of our meeting place was flat and held a volleyball court with a chain link fence around it where the young men played. As she looked up, she saw a man in a white robe walking around on top of the church. She knew instantly that it was an angel.

"Lord, I am sorry I questioned You," she said, and walked back in and stood by the door. I began the service. Suddenly everything became quiet. The young men had left, though no one had said a word to them.

The next day, the man who owned the gambling hall

approached me and jabbed his finger at my chest. "You finally turned us in," he said bitterly. "Your God wasn't big enough to protect you."

"I didn't turn you in," I said.

"Yes, you did," he said. "My boys saw that policeman on top of the roof last night."

I was puzzled, and I went home and asked Donna what had happened. She told me about the man on the roof. I told her the gambling hall owner thought it was a soldier. She laughed.

"If it had been a soldier, I would have told him to get off our roof," she said. "But I saw a man in a white robe. I believe he was an angel."

Occurrences like that were common in those days, because we were in the thick of enemy territory, bringing a message of hope, salvation, healing, and the baptism in the Holy Spirit. The more trouble the devil caused us, the more the Lord blessed the work.

One Friday night as I was preaching to a church almost completely full of young people, a man walked into the building and interrupted me.

"This man is hypnotizing you!" he loudly told the people. "You had better get up and leave."

Most people stayed, but some got up and walked out. Then the man left, and I continued my sermon, though we were all a little bewildered by what had happened.

A few days later, I was walking down the street, and I came face-to-face with the very man who had made the announcement. I recognized him now. He was the brother of a warlord. He looked me squarely in the face with fury emanating from his eyes.

"Preacher, I give you thirty days to pack up your benches and get out of this neighborhood," he threatened.

I knew he could do me great physical harm, but I had to meet his challenge.

"Sir, I give you thirty days to repent!" I said, and walked away. He was stunned by my boldness.

I went directly to the church and knelt. "Lord," I said quietly, "You heard what I said to the man. He has power in this neighborhood and could have me killed, if he wanted. Please bail me out! Save this man before the thirty days are over."

A week went by and nothing happened. Then another week went by, and I learned that this man owned the gambling hall down the street. It was his livelihood. When our church had rented the villa nearby, many of the local young people got saved and quit gambling, putting a crimp in his profits. He had gotten so desperate for business that he came personally to disrupt our meeting.

Without my doing anything but praying, the government came and locked up his gambling hall, claiming he was doing illegal things. He thought I had reported him, but I had only spoken to God about it. In abject need of hope, he decided to come to the meeting one Friday night. This time he sat in a seat in the back and listened. When the altar call was given, he walked down the aisle and knelt at the altar. I knelt beside him and led him in the sinner's prayer. Joy filled his heart and beamed from his face. He looked like a completely different person than the one who had threatened me weeks earlier. I hugged him, and he embraced me back. The next morning he bought a Bible, and I signed it for him and wrote down the date of his conversion. It was less than thirty days after our confrontation in the street.

While God worked in many lives, our task remained difficult, and I was often discouraged. I didn't feel that I was seeing the kind of signs and wonders that I had read about in the Book of Acts. *I wanted more,* and I knew that much more was needed to win the Middle East.

HE WROTE BACK TO ME, "ELIAS, STICK WITH IT. GOD HAS USED YOU, AND HE WILL CONTINUE TO USE YOU."

"Lord," I often prayed with tears, "if I am baptized in the Holy Spirit, where are the miracles that should follow the ministry?"

I did not receive an immediate answer. During one particularly troubling season, doubt stole into my mind concerning my experience with the Holy Spirit. I wrote a letter to my mission director in California telling him I wanted to resign.

"We are seeing people saved," I wrote, "but nobody is receiving the baptism in the Holy Spirit."

He wrote back to me, "Elias, stick with it. God has used you, and He will continue to use you."

I was happy to hear from him, but it did not answer my questions, so I decided to go on a ten-day fast. I locked myself in a room up in the mountains. I drank only water for five days and sought the Lord constantly, praying and reading the Bible. Then I had a little bowl of soup and went five more days with only water. After that, I went back to the church, and the Lord said, "OK. I will show you signs and miracles."

The first miracle happened to Mary, one of the women of our church. She had a skin disease all over her body and was a new bride to a soldier in the army. Though they were both Christians already in name, she came to our church and was truly born again. Then we prayed for her, and the Lord healed her of the skin disease. Her husband was thankful, but he was also afraid that she would join our church, so he forbade her to come again.

When she didn't show up for a while, I investigated why. When I learned that her husband was keeping her from coming to church, I met with him. After talking with him for a while, I looked him in the eyes. "If you do not let your wife come to church, the same disease she had will come upon you, to show you that God is real in this church," I said.

Twenty-four hours later, on a Wednesday night, he and his wife came to church. His skin was covered in a rash. "Please, pray for me," he asked, almost trembling with fear.

I laid my hands on him and prayed, and the next day he was completely back to normal.

I knew God was releasing miracle power through our church—exactly what it would take to win the Middle East for Christ. Still, I hungered to see people filled with the Holy Spirit as a regular part of church life, so I took an unusual step for Beirut churches. I planned a revival at the church, with evening services every night for a week. An evangelist came, and the Lord used him to bring twelve people into the baptism of the Holy Spirit. In other parts of the world, twelve people would not have been considered much. But for us, it was a breakthrough, and the news spread to every evangelical church in town.

WE PRAYED WITH AUTHORITY AND BELIEVED, AND A FEW DAYS LATER WE RECEIVED NEWS THAT THE GIRL WAS RELEASED FROM THE HOSPITAL, FREE OF LEUKEMIA.

Those people who were thirsty for the power of God came and were also baptized in the Holy Spirit. As God displayed His power and brought peace to people, the Pentecostal message gained credibility. In years past, Pentecostals had earned a negative reputation in Beirut, because they had been unwise in their conduct. They had left a stigma on the Spirit-filled message, and none of their churches survived very long. Aside from the two churches I had planted and the mission I was saved in, there were now no other Pentecostal churches in the city, to my knowledge. I realized that we had a chance to redefine the message of salvation for a generation that had little knowledge of it. People saw that faith in Christ meant something other than following the rituals of a church. It meant miracle power for everyday situations. As we continued to pray, the signs and wonders also continued, and soon we had gained a reputation as a place where people could turn for healing when doctors had given up on them.

My brother-in-law Abraham came to me one day.

"My thirteen-year-old cousin is dying of leukemia," he said. "The doctors don't give her much hope. Her parents are not believers, but they are willing to let you come and pray for her. Will you do it?"

We went to the hospital, and as we entered the room the Lord gave me assurance that He would heal her. We prayed with authority and believed, and a few days later we received news that the girl was released from the hospital, free of leukemia.

But with miracles came greater opposition, much of it from Christians who did not believe in the power of the Holy Spirit the way we were preaching it. Our meetings sometimes lasted two hours, so people who went to other churches with one-hour meetings had the chance to attend our services for the sole purpose of interrupting and causing trouble. One cold January evening, I was preaching, and we had all the doors and windows closed to keep what little heat we had inside. A young man, a stranger to me, got up and walked out of the building in the middle of my sermon. Half a minute later, a terrible odor filled the small auditorium, and we could not continue the service. The young man had set off a stink bomb. We opened the windows because the smell was unbearable, and that let in the cold. Everyone had to go home. We discovered that the perpetrator was a member of a neighboring evangelical church that did not agree with our teaching.

Soon a fresh wave of military violence would visit the country again, and the dangers of living in Beirut would increase so much that stink bombs seemed like child's play.

~ᴄ~   Chapter 9   ~ᴄ~

THE HOLY SPIRIT MOVES IN THE MIDDLE EAST

WITH THE HELP of our church in Beirut, the Charismatic movement came to the Middle East in the early 1970s. The movement had already gained steam in the United States and elsewhere, but was almost unknown in the Middle East. Christians in the Middle East had never heard the new Scripture songs that were becoming popular, so we translated them into Arabic and introduced them to the evangelical churches in Lebanon. Everything we did seemed to yield amazing results that reverberated across the region. Our church put on the first Charismatic summer camp in Lebanon for people from Syria, Lebanon, Jordan, and Egypt. We brought in speakers from America and the Middle East in the summer of 1970 and met in the beautiful mountains of Lebanon.

The entire week was like heaven on earth. Many people came thinking they would have a nice vacation in Lebanon, and they ended up getting saved, healed, and baptized in the Holy Spirit. Today, some of those people are in full-time ministry in Jordan, Syria, Egypt, and Lebanon. One of them was an engineer from Damascus who went into full-time ministry with his wife and children. Another man came from Jordan, and he later became the senior pastor of the largest church in Amman. At the camp he received the baptism in the Holy Spirit, and his father's heart and back were healed. When people left, they took the Scripture songs to churches across the Arabic-speaking world, and those simple tunes transformed the way congregations worshiped.

MANY PEOPLE CAME THINKING THEY WOULD HAVE A NICE VACATION IN LEBANON, AND THEY ENDED UP GETTING SAVED, HEALED, AND BAPTIZED IN THE HOLY SPIRIT.

Our church flourished, too, even in the midst of the continual opposition. Even though our church developed a reputation as a place where signs and wonders and healings took place regularly, the enemy was still at work to destroy our effectiveness. The opposition grew as more and more people began to accept our Pentecostal message. But in spite of the enemy's tactics to stymie our efforts, God continued to bring people to Him.

One day I met a young man named Raffoul in whom I saw great potential for the kingdom of God. He came from a traditional Christian background, but God moved on his heart, and he became a faithful attendee of our church and Sunday school. One night we were praying for Raffoul and others to receive the baptism in the Holy Spirit, and the Lord touched him so powerfully that he could no longer speak Arabic. He spoke in tongues for hours and stumbled around like a drunken man when he tried to walk. We had to drive him home, and when his mother saw him, she thought I had hypnotized him. She forbade him to come to our church, but I would not give up on him. Once a week we met secretly, sitting in my car for an hour or two while I taught him the Bible.

When he turned eighteen and gained the right to come to church on his own, I told him, "I am not going to meet with you anymore. You have to come to church openly."

"Are you willing to face the reprisal of my mother?" he asked. "If you are, I will come."

It was Friday night—almost time for the youth meeting. Our decision would have consequences soon.

"If you are willing to come, I am willing to face her," I said.

The service began at 7:00 p.m., but we met for prayer at 6:00 p.m. When I arrived, Raffoul was inside the yard with his mother. I had to pass them to open the door of the church.

"Don't you go in," his mother said to him, but he entered anyway. His mother followed us in. Once inside, Raffoul and I got down on our knees to pray, and the minute he knelt, he began to speak in tongues. His mother looked at me with alarm.

"You need to loose him," she said, and raised her right hand to slap me.

"He is loose," I said. "You need to be loosed."

She tried to slap me but couldn't bring her hand toward me.

"Set him loose," she said again.

BY 1975, CIVIL WAR HAD BROKEN OUT. NO QUARTER WAS SAFE.

"He is loose," I repeated, and she raised her hand again to slap me, but could not. Instead, she found the kitchen, poured a glass of water, and brought it in to dump on her son to startle him out of the trance she thought he was in.

"Loose him," she said to me again. Just as she was about to splash the water on his face, he spoke to her in Arabic.

"Woman, I am loosed. This is the power of God. You need to be saved."

She looked at me, eyes wide, then back at her son. She set the glass down, walked out, and never opposed him again. Over the years he has become a "Timothy" to me, and he became the pastor in one of the fastest-growing churches in Lowell, Massachusetts. His mother, who moved with him to Massachusetts, not only quit opposing him but would kiss me on the cheek whenever I visited them.

But in spite of the way our church was flourishing, the political situation in Lebanon grew increasingly tense and volatile. Under normal circumstances the government was divided among the various religious groups: the president was always an Eastern Catholic, the prime minister a Sunni Muslim, the speaker of Parliament a Shiite Muslim. But Palestinian refugees, who were almost all Sunni Muslims, had grown so powerful in south Lebanon and in west Beirut where our church was located that the area was destabilized and unsafe. Key government leaders feared that the Palestinian refugees would eventually overthrow the present government. Accusations flew, and frictions heightened between every political and religious group.

By 1975, civil war had broken out. No quarter was safe. The government was divided, and the Palestinians took power. Yasser Arafat took control of certain territories. People could not go into the streets for fear of violence. Many people on both sides of the conflict were kidnapped and brutally murdered.

My denomination grew nervous about my presence in Lebanon. My family and I had returned twice to the United States to raise money, always coming back to Lebanon and always finding it more dangerous than before. At one point our denominational leaders asked me to be their international evangelist, traveling the world to hold special meetings at their foreign mission stations. I would be stationed in South America. It was a tempting offer—and certainly my family would have been safer. But they also said they would close the work in Lebanon completely. "I'm sorry—no," I told them. "My heart is in the Middle East." When they saw my determination, they allowed us to go back to Lebanon for five more years with their support.

Even as the violence escalated, the Lord laid it on my heart to start a Bible school. I remodeled the old building we were in. With its high-ceilinged rooms I was able to put another floor in, adding bathrooms and bedrooms to create dormitories. We now had a Bible school and housing to accommodate twelve students. Soon, young people came from Iraq, Egypt, Jordan, Syria, and Lebanon. Astonishingly, they all boarded peacefully in the same building.

THE SITUATION HAD TURNED FROM A POLITICAL WAR INTO A RELIGIOUS ONE BETWEEN MUSLIMS AND CHRISTIANS, AN UNFORTUNATE AND GRIEVOUS TURN OF EVENTS.

During our three-year program they learned Greek and Hebrew, doctrine, homiletics, and all the other standard Bible school subjects. Our professors were former missionaries from England and the United States. We made history by opening the first full-gospel Bible school in the city of Beirut, and, to top it off, the curriculum and classroom teaching were entirely in Arabic.

I worked hard to make the Bible school work, but the logistics became especially tricky when the country broke into active civil war. We planned our first Bible school graduation in the midst of the military clashes taking place all around us. Officials from our denomination had been invited to participate in the graduation, but the day before it was to take place, the director of foreign missions called me from Athens.

"I'm sorry, but I and the group with me won't be able to come to Lebanon due to the situation," he said. "In fact, we have decided that you should close the work in Lebanon and take your family back to the United States. We want you to evacuate as soon as possible, because the situation could become worse."

I understood his concerns, but I was not about to leave Lebanon. We proceeded with the graduation and had an exciting ceremony. Under the sound of bombs and gunfire, we laid hands on our students for the first time and set them apart for the ministry.

But his advice to close the work and head for safer ground began to make more sense as the violence became less predictable and less contained, and as my children were threatened. My children were teenagers now and had refused to stay in the United States after our last furlough. The girls especially wanted to finish college in Lebanon. But my commitment to stay and spread the gospel in Beirut was increasingly at odds with their safety. The situation had turned from a political war into a religious one between Muslims and Christians, an unfortunate and grievous turn of events. As a result, it was difficult for my kids even to attend school.

One day Tim, who had just turned sixteen, took our car to pick up Rebecca from college. To get there, he had to drive through Palestinian-controlled areas full of road-blocks and civilians carrying automatic weapons. On his way, he saw his friend Bahjat, a Muslim boy, standing on his balcony.

"Do you want to take a ride with me?" he shouted, and Bahjat, eager for the chance to ride with a friend, ran down-stairs and got into the car.

They made it safely to the college, picked up Rebecca, and headed home. But they were stopped at a roadblock in a Muslim area.

"Show me your IDs," the armed man said. Tim and Rebecca handed him their cards. By law, people had to carry IDs that stated their religious affiliation. When the man saw they were Christians, he gave them a suspicious glance.

"We will keep these two, but you can go," he said to Bahjat.

"No, let them go with me," Bahjat said. "They mean nothing to you. They are harmless."

Bahjat was only a teenager, but he was the son of a promi-nent Muslim family, and he used his influence.

The guards consulted among themselves, pointing at the vehicle and at my children.

"We'll let you go, but we're keeping the car," they finally said.

"No," Bahjat snapped. "And if you don't let them go with their car, you are going to be sorry."

The guards, knowing he might not be bluffing, gave in and let them go, but my children came home shaking. I knew then it was time for us to leave Lebanon.

We prayed constantly and kept the church going as we made plans to leave. People were coming and getting saved at the weekend services, but during the week my family and I escaped to a mountain getaway where we had a mission station. There we could sleep in peace without the sound of bombs going off throughout the city, which often kept us awake all night. Our habit was to drive to the mountains early Monday morning, then come back down on Wednesday for our midweek Bible study. The road leading up the mountain was dangerous because of the war, and there were plenty of roadblocks and kidnappings along the way.

To make our situation in Beirut worse, the corner minimarket just beneath our second-story flat kept getting bombed. The owner was a Shiite Muslim, and he apparently had highly motivated enemies. Three times within one month, explosives ripped through his store. The first time it shattered every bit of glass in our flat. Our beds shook, and the kids were badly frightened. I was too, but I still believed that things would get better.

One Sunday evening after the service the children pleaded with me, "Dad, let's go to the mountains tonight, not tomorrow morning." The bombing always started at night, so I understood their fear, but I was reluctant to go. Still, their entreaties touched my heart, so I agreed. Our neighbor Mustafa, who lived beneath us, always taunted us when we got ready to go up the mountain.

"Your God is not going to get you up there tonight," he said, as he always did.

"Our God will take us," I promised. It was our ongoing dialogue.

We loaded our little station wagon and set out, but as we approached the foot of the mountain, the man two cars ahead of us began arguing with the terrorists at the road-block. Their words became so sharp that I thought they would shoot him. I didn't want my children to witness it, nor did I want any trouble because we were Christians.

"I think we had better turn around and go back home," I said, to everyone's disappointment. I turned the car around and drove home as fast as I could. When Mustafa saw us, he said, "See, I knew your God couldn't get you up there."

"Mustafa, there is a good reason we didn't get to go up there today," I said, not bothering to relate what had happened at the roadblock. I walked into our house, and to my surprise the kitchen floor was covered in water. The water cistern overhead had broken. Donna, who had been drenched by a waterfall of it, called for me, and I quickly called for Mustafa to help. He was astonished at what had happened.

"Mr. Malki, your God knows what He is doing," he said as we bailed water. "If you had gone up the mountain, your house would have been ruined, and mine would have been ruined, too."

The next morning we learned that people at the road-block where we had turned the car around were kidnapped and murdered.

It was impossible to get airline tickets to the States. Every flight was sold out. Americans, Europeans, and Lebanese who could afford it were fleeing Beirut in droves. Frustrated, I had to wait. Half the city was shut down, and you couldn't even buy bread except when the bakery happened to open. Normally, my son Danny, a fourteen-year-old, fetched the bread for us from the bakery across the street where people lined up to buy pita bread, but the bakery had been closed for days. One day he noticed it was open, so he and a friend went. While there, someone did something to upset the owner, and he reached for his gun and fired at the crowd of customers in the store. Danny and his friend ran outside as fast as they could, even stepping on top of people. When Donna heard the gunfire from across the street, she ran outside but saw nothing.

I PUT THINGS IN ORDER, PLACED THE CHURCH IN THE HANDS OF ONE OF OUR GRADUATES, DROVE TO AMMAN, LEFT MY CAR WITH ONE OF MY CONVERTS THERE, AND FLEW TO THE UNITED STATES.

"Elias," she said, "something is wrong. I can't see Daniel."

She ran to the door and opened it, and Danny and his friend fell inside. God had spared their lives.

It was time for extreme measures. I drove Donna, the children, and my father, who was old and feeble and was visiting from the States, to Amman, Jordan, the only airport that had available flights out. They boarded and left for America, and I went back to our apartment with Danny, who was finishing school in just two weeks. As soon as he finished school, I secured him a ticket out of Beirut, and he flew to Los Angeles alone.

I stayed behind and kept the church going. Some people left the city. Others stayed, and services continued as usual.

Not a day went by that I didn't anticipate violence against me from those who hated Christianity. But the Lord gave me courage to stand in the middle of the crisis. I put things in order, placed the church in the hands of one of our graduates, drove to Amman, left my car with one of my converts there, and flew to the United States.

When I arrived in Los Angeles, I met with the director of foreign missions.

"As far as we are concerned the work in Lebanon is closed," he said. "We cannot help you financially any more. We will carry you and your family to the end of the year—three months from now. Then you are on your own."

I was not willing to give up the work in Lebanon. The people there needed us. But soon God would open a new, unexpected door, which would broaden my ministry far beyond Lebanon and allow me to preach the gospel directly to millions all over the Middle East.

~c~ Chapter 10 ~c~

A NEW WAY—BROADCASTING
THE GOOD NEWS

WITHOUT THE SUPPORT of our denomination, I scrambled to find finances to keep the ministry in Lebanon going. At the advice of Jack Hayford, pastor of The Church On The Way and founder of the King's College and Seminary in Van Nuys, we formed a nonprofit corporation called Elias Malki Middle East Gospel Outreach. Jack, Charles Flynn, Donna, and I were the founding board members.

We also started a nonprofit corporation called Community International to help the poor in Lebanon and other Middle Eastern countries. In 1977 we sent a twenty-foot container of food to Lebanon's civil war victims. This opened a significant door for sharing the gospel, because the food was distributed without regard to religion. We sent another container of medical equipment to a hospital in south Lebanon and shipped forty tons of dried milk to the needy in Egypt. The shipments foreshadowed the change that was coming to my ministry, which would blanket the Middle East with the gospel.

I felt the change coming. I could sense in my spirit that I was in a moment of crisis when the old must be left behind and a new thing brought forth. My heart told me that if the gospel was going to make any inroads in the Middle East, it needed to happen on a much broader scale. It bothered me that we were only reaching people in historical churches—Catholics, Protestants, and Greek Orthodox. We were not reaching the masses of the Middle East—the Arab Muslims.

"How can I reach these people?" I cried out to God one day in prayer.

In my spirit, I heard Him answer, "You are twenty years behind the times. Use radio and television. They are tools to bring the gospel to those who have never heard."

I instantly recalled the old *Lutheran Hour* broadcasts I had worked for in 1951 when I was a new Christian. I did some research and learned the *Lutheran Hour* was still broadcasting weekly from a station in Monte Carlo. I wrote them a letter and explained that I wanted to buy airtime. They sent an application for me to fill out. One of the questions was, "Do you speak in tongues?" I was honest and answered, "Yes." I never heard from them again. Disappointed, I pressed on without them.

It was all but impossible to buy time on any Middle Eastern radio station, because the airwaves were controlled by governments, and the governments were controlled by people hostile to Christ. Then one day as I was praying, the Lord said, "Go to the island of Cyprus." I knew next to nothing about Cyprus. I had spent one night there after evacuating Lebanon in 1967 during the Six-Day War. Going further back, I knew from the Bible account that Cyprus was the home of Barnabas, and the whole island had been Christianized after Paul and Barnabas preached there and performed miracles, and the governor had believed. Cyprus became the first Christian government, and the people there were now mostly Greek Orthodox.

On faith alone, I flew from the United States to Cyprus, not knowing a soul. I checked myself into a hotel and opened the telephone directory to look for evangelical churches. Most of the churches were Greek Orthodox, but my eyes fell on the words *Community Church*. I called the number, and a man answered.

THEN ONE DAY AS I WAS PRAYING, THE LORD SAID, "GO TO THE ISLAND OF CYPRUS."

"Hello," he said. "This is the Community Church. My name is Hercules. Can I help you?"

I was amazed to hear of someone who actually went by the name of Hercules, but I regained my composure and said, "My name is Elias Malki. I am an American Lebanese. I was sent by the Holy Spirit to see if I can buy airtime on radio to preach the gospel to the Arab world. Can you help me?"

Hercules, it turned out, was a born-again Christian, the general manager of the island's main airport, and the head elder of the Anglican community church. He was influential on the island, but he discouraged me from my task.

"It is impossible to buy time here," he said. "The radio is government controlled."

"Can I meet you?" I asked, undeterred. "I will buy your lunch."

GOD HAD BEGUN A NEW WORK IN THE MIDDLE EAST, AND THOUGH SMALL, IT WOULD GROW QUICKLY.

He agreed, and he came to the hotel to have lunch with me. After we had talked, he nodded slowly.

"The best thing I can do is to introduce you to my good friend and schoolmate who is the general manager of the radio station," he said.

That same afternoon I met with the general manager, a short, red-haired man. Two hours later, we signed the first contract in the history of the Middle East and possibly the world to preach the full gospel on radio in the Arabic language. The *Good News* program was born; it would air on Wednesday and Friday nights at ten o'clock. It would last half an hour and be completely in Arabic.

I was thrilled to have come all that way to find a wide open door for ministry. At the time, few preachers even in the United States were on the radio. Now I had the opportunity to take the gospel into new territory. But the station didn't give me unrestricted access to their listeners. They appointed a man who spoke Arabic to censor every program before it went on the air.

"We don't want any fanatical preaching," the general manager told me. "If we feel it is fanatical, we won't put it on the air."

I agreed to his terms. And they stuck me with the bill, so I had to pay one hundred dollars to have every program censored.

Jubilant, I took the contract home to California and showed it to my friend Chuck Smith of Calvary Chapel in Costa Mesa. Chuck not only looked over the contract, but he also gave me a check for two thousand dollars to pay for the first two months. In his recording room at Calvary Chapel I recorded the first *Good News* radio program. I sent eight programs to Cyprus one month in advance. God had begun a new work in the Middle East, and though small, it would grow quickly.

For six months I abided by the agreement not to be too "fanatical." I preached the gospel, but I did not operate in any of the gifts of the Spirit. Then one day while recording a program, I decided not to quench the Holy Spirit. I took a chance. As I opened my mouth, the Holy Spirit gave me a word of knowledge, and I allowed my tongue to speak His words.

"There is a man listening," I said. "You are seventy years old. You just came back from the doctor's office. You have smoked all your life. Your lungs are full of cancer. The doctors could not help you. You are depressed. If you will get up from your chair right now and put one hand on the radio and the other hand on your chest and pray this prayer after me, God will heal you from the cancer."

I began to pray, "O God. I know You love me. I know You can heal me. I know You are able. In the name of Jesus the Christ, the Son of the living God, heal me now. Amen."

I stopped and thought, *Is this fanatical? Will the station put this on the air?* I didn't know, but I shipped the tape to Cyprus anyway. And I waited.

Two weeks later, I received a letter from Baghdad, Iraq:

> Thank you for the *Good News* program. I am the man you were referring to. I put my hand on the radio and on my chest, and for the first time I called on the name of Jesus the Son of God. I am healed! Will you send me a Bible? I believed in Jesus before as a prophet, but now I believe He is the Son of the living God. I am now a Christian.

I was overjoyed. To me, that was the true beginning of the *Good News* program. God had used the radio ministry to heal a man in a place where I had never preached in person.

Then I visited Cyprus on my way to Beirut so I could stop by the station and pay my bill for airtime. I went inside as usual to see the general manager, but this time he was unhappy to see me.

"Reverend Malki, I believe we agreed that we don't want fanatical preaching. What is this 'Put your hand on the radio and put your hand on your chest and pray with me' business? We asked you not to do that because 99 percent of our listeners are Arab people, and they don't believe like we believe. We don't want them to boycott our station."

He told me that when that particular tape had arrived in Cyprus, the man who normally censored the program was on vacation. A substitute censor listened to it and aired it, but our usual censor happened to be listening at the time my program was aired, and he came straight to the general manager and told him about it.

The general manager had the same mind-set as many Christians in historical churches in the Middle East. He didn't care to reach out to Arabs. For centuries the Greek Orthodox and others had suffered under the tyranny of Arab governments, and so they harbored a hatred and fear of Muslims. They lacked faith that God could change Arabs.

From that moment forward, the number of signs and wonders in my ministry increased exponentially.

"Listen," I said to the general manager, "God loves everybody, including Arabs, and they can be changed by the gospel just as well as you and I can."

I could see this was making him angry, and he began to bluster at me, so I pulled from my pocket the letter I had received from the man in Baghdad. The interpreter read the letter for him. Just then, the general manager's secretary came in and asked, "What kind of drink can I offer you, sir? Would you like something cold or something hot—tea or coffee?"

Before I could answer, the Holy Spirit gave me a word of knowledge.

"You have back problems, don't you?" I asked.

She looked at me, puzzled.

"Yes," she admitted.

"Can I pray for you? God will heal you," I said.

The general manager was ready to call my bluff. He stood up.

"If you can heal her I will believe," he said.

"I cannot heal her," I said, "but God can."

I asked her again, "Can I pray for you?"

"Are you a representative of Jesus Christ?" she asked.

"Yes, I am," I said.

"Where is your beard and black robe?" she asked. The priests in Cyprus wore beards and long black robes.

"I don't need a beard and a black robe," I said. "But I can tell you this: this morning when you came to work you had such pain that you stopped by the pharmacy, and the pharmacist gave you a different pain pill than you normally take."

"Pray for me," she said. I laid my hands on her, prayed, and she was straightened out and completely healed. I turned to the general manager.

"Do you believe?" I said.

"Tomorrow when she comes in without any pain, then I will believe," he said.

The next day came, and she had no pain. As I visited Cyprus over the next five years, she remained completely healed. The general manager and I became friends, and he stopped censoring my programs. From that moment forward, the number of signs and wonders in my ministry increased exponentially.

While I was busy launching a radio ministry in Cyprus, I was also still overseeing the church in Lebanon during the time of political crisis there. Every three months I flew in and stayed for two or three months to encourage the people. I did this for five years, and the Lord blessed us with many new converts. Some were baptized with the Holy Spirit.

One night I arrived in Beirut at 11:00 p.m. and took a taxi to the apartment we kept, which was adjacent to the church. I was exhausted and went to my bedroom to sleep. Then the phone rang.

"We know who you are," said the man on the other end of the line. "You are a CIA agent. You are a Jewish spy. We've got your number. You'll be next."

Then there was silence. I put the receiver down and tried to sleep but was so afraid that instead I called on the Lord. Our front door had no latch on the inside, and I could not prevent people from getting in. But I had nowhere else to go. Violence was not new to me—I had had close calls before, but never a direct death threat. There was no law and order in Beirut, no one to whom I could appeal. Even the church's telephone line had been stolen by terrorists, who used it with impunity. Power resided in the hands of those groups who had the worst intentions. I didn't sleep much that night.

When I awoke, I went to see my distant cousin and told him about the phone call. He was a nominal Christian and an official member of the government in that area.

"Do you have any kind of weapon to protect yourself?" he asked.

"No," I said. He tried to hand me his machine gun.

"No, thank you," I said. "I really don't need it."

He insisted, but I wouldn't take the weapon.

"The Lord and His angels will take care of me," I said. "I just thought I would let you know what happened."

He shrugged, probably thinking I was an impractical fool. I stayed in Beirut for three months, and I never received another threat.

In 1981, the civil situation in Lebanon worsened beyond what I thought possible. Israel moved in and took over the country. American President Ronald Reagan had to send the Marines to give Yasser Arafat and his group safe passage out of the country. Violence and mayhem increased tenfold. Lebanon became a boiling pot of conflict and chaos.

Donna and I decided to return one last time to gather our personal belongings from the apartment, sell what we could, and give the rest away. The young man who took care of the church had escaped to the east side of Beirut, which was safer and where most Christians had decamped. The members of our congregation had all fled. The neighborhood, once a bustling marketplace of diverse people, had fallen quiet.

Donna and I cleared out our home, packed some items in trunks, and took the trunks to the pier to be shipped home. We handed over the apartment to the owner and surrendered the church building we had rented. I loaded the homemade benches into a truck to take them to the east side of Beirut. Then I remembered the steeple we had built in front of the church. I looked up—it was still there. Atop the steeple was a cross, which proclaimed that the power and mercy of Jesus were available in that place. The steeple also housed a church bell, which rang out when we had services, a symbol of the joy to be found in the gospel.

"Hold on a moment," I told Donna as we finished loading up. I found a ladder, climbed up, and took the church bell down. But I left the cross on top of the steeple. We might not be there, but people could still look to the sky and see silhouetted against the smoke and dust of war the eternal sign of hope.

We did not lose any of our belongings, and nobody interfered with us as we evacuated—a miracle in itself. Donna and I left Lebanon for the safety of the United States. Our work as pastors in Beirut was over, but my ministry to the Middle East had just begun.

Chapter 11

BEHIND CLOSED BORDERS

F OR THE NEXT few years, any visit to Lebanon was like a strategic strike into enemy territory. In 1982, as America was negotiating with Israel for Israel to pull out of Lebanon, a suicide bomber in Beirut killed more than two hundred forty U.S. Marines who were stationed there to keep peace. It was a terrible and disturbing event, and I decided to help in the aftermath. Comedian Bob Hope, singer Pat Boone, and Jeff Johnson, pastor of Calvary Chapel in Downey, California, decided to go with me to comfort the Marines. Because of the danger, Pat Boone and Bob Hope decided not to go, but Jeff and I pressed on and went together to Amman a few days after the bombing.

We caught a flight to Beirut, which normally would have

carried at least a hundred people; this time we were the only passengers on the plane. As we were airborne, my concern for Jeff grew because he was an American traveling to a country where the United States was, to put it mildly, not fully appreciated. I wondered if terrorists might try to pick us up at the airport and hold us for ransom. Just setting foot in Lebanon put us at risk of being kidnapped.

I opened my Bible, and my eyes fell on Psalm 42:5: "Why art thou cast down O my soul?" That was how I felt. My soul was downcast. I read on: "Therefore will I remember thee from the land of Jordan..." (v. 6).

We were still in the air over Jordan. It was like I was living out the psalm, remembering God from the land of Jordan. The psalmist continued, "...and of the Hermonites."

I looked out the window and soon saw Mt. Hermon. Then I came to verse 11:

"Why art thou cast down, O my soul?...hope thou in God: for I shall yet praise him, who is the health of my countenance, and my God."

The fear that had gripped me began to recede, and I knew God was going to take care of us. I shared the verses with Jeff, and he seemed unperturbed. His life was more in danger than mine, but he had peace about our journey.

We landed in Beirut, and the airport appeared to be abandoned. Our footsteps echoed through empty hallways. We found a taxi to take us half an hour away to the mountain where I had reserved rooms in a mission home.

"Don't say a word," I told Jeff, just to be careful. I didn't want him to advertise that he was an American.

The taxi took us through streets and alleys, and we couldn't be sure if the driver meant us good or ill. His route was erratic, through back streets and alleyways. I couldn't figure out if he was taking us through known safe routes or bringing us to kidnappers who had worked out a deal with him earlier in case he was lucky enough to find Americans at the airport. His eyes flicked here and there, glancing at us in the rearview mirror. There was no way of knowing his intentions. Jeff and I prayed under our breath, and the Lord kept reminding me, "Hope in the Lord."

When the driver finally delivered us to our destination, my heart was flooded with relief. God had again accompanied us into the battle zone.

THE FEAR THAT HAD GRIPPED ME BEGAN TO RECEDE, AND I KNEW GOD WAS GOING TO TAKE CARE OF US.

The next day we called the commander of the Marines and made ourselves available for prayer and services there on Sunday. The commander invited us to meet with him, and he introduced us to the Catholic and Protestant chaplains. We spent three days with the troops, and Jeff and I spoke messages that were carried on closed-circuit television to every barrack. Some of the men came to the small chapel and, for the first time, I preached to soldiers. They were still reeling from the bombing that had taken the lives of their comrades. We also visited hospitals and prayed for the sick. In the dark days following the bombing, we were happy to lend what help we could, knowing the heavy toll the Marines had suffered.

About that time a minister named George Otis put a mobile television station in Lebanon and began broadcasting. He asked me to host a television program, and though the timing didn't feel right, the idea piqued my interest. I couldn't put it out of my mind. He soon sold the station to Pat Robertson, founder of the Christian Broadcasting Network based in Virginia Beach.

I happened to be traveling to the Holy Land with a group of people when the transition of ownership was taking place. Someone told me that Pat was on the plane. I looked around and found him, sat down beside him, and we talked for hours.

God had taught me... how to put together a program under the strict direction of the Holy Spirit instead of using my own wisdom.

"Elias," he asked at one point, "would you be willing to do an Arabic program similar to *The 700 Club* to be aired from south Lebanon and broadcast all over the region?"

I was so grateful to hear him say that. "The Lord has spoken to me to go on television," I said, "but I need to check with my board first."

Back in the United States, I met with the board. They agreed I should move ahead, but then the mobile station was bombed. Pat didn't waste any time: he rebuilt it and changed the name to Middle East Television. I accepted his invitation and flew to Virginia Beach to record the first *Good News* television program with the same crew that did *The 700 Club*. My daughter Ruth became my producer and worked there in Virginia Beach, in charge of the Arabic translation of *The 700 Club*.

I taped five programs that day, and they aired all over Galilee, northern Israel, north Jordan, Syria, and portions of Egypt and Lebanon. From 1982 to 1994 the *Good News* program was the only Arabic Christian TV program in the Middle East. It also aired on secular stations in southern California and in Detroit, places with large Arab populations.

God had taught me with the *Good News* radio program how to be sensitive in everything I said and how to put together a program under the strict direction of the Holy Spirit instead of using my own wisdom. I knew that was the only way it would touch people's hearts. With the television program, I used the same approach. I did not target any one religion. Rather, I paid constant attention to the guard God put over my mouth so that I would speak to viewers of all backgrounds. But I did not compromise the name of Jesus. I spoke the Word as it is in the Bible.

Soon, the program had gained a significant viewership, and I could not travel in the Middle East without being greeted by people in public places. Many asked for prayer. Others told me their testimonies. I was thankful, not for the recognition, but because it meant people were watching the program, and they considered me a trustworthy, credible person.

The opportunities to preach by radio and television kept coming. One day Pat Robertson called and told me he was in touch with a group in Lebanon. He wanted to offer them a radio transmitter and antenna as a gift, on the condition that they allow Christian radio programs to be aired.

"Elias, I'd like you to go to Lebanon and meet with them," Pat said. "Mail service is unreliable, so I want you to deliver your radio program directly to them on audiocassette so we can begin broadcasting."

By that time the airport in Lebanon was completely closed, and the only way in was by car through Israel, which still controlled Lebanon. The situation there had not improved one iota. It was risky even to enter the country, which was an ongoing war zone. Jeff Johnson again volunteered to accompany me—the only person I knew who was brave enough. We found ourselves back in the Middle East for what I hoped would be a straightforward project, but this time things didn't go smoothly. From the moment we arrived, the atmosphere seemed tense, the situation on the ground messy and dangerous. We sensed that only the careful guidance of the Holy Spirit would carry us safely through. We took a taxi to the border of Lebanon, but the guards would not allow Jeff to enter. I tried to prevail on them, but they could not be persuaded. However, I was welcome to enter because I was born in Lebanon. I had to continue on, and Jeff and I had to separate.

"I don't know what to do," I told Jeff. "You can go back home, or you can stay until I come back. In either case, I'll see you when I get back."

We parted, and with the package of *Good News* programs on audiocassette clutched under my arm, I entered the no-man's-land between the Israeli and Lebanese borders. It was a barren stretch of land where nobody lived or worked. A road ran straight from one side to the other, but public transportation was not allowed there, only military or United Nations vehicles. I walked half a mile on foot over the dusty road with nothing to contemplate but the sky and the dangers I might confront on the other side.

THE LORD SAID, "GO TO THE FRONT AND TALK TO THE MAN IN CHARGE ABOUT YOUR SITUATION."

Just inside Lebanon, I took a two-hour public bus ride to the city of Sidon. The civil war raged fiercely around us. Snipers' bullets flew overhead constantly. I heard them whizzing by as the bus bumped and rattled down the pockmarked road. I arrived safely in Sidon, but the roads between Sidon and Beirut were closed because of lawlessness, vicious kidnappings, and roadblocks. The only way to Beirut was by a three-hour boat ride. I found the dock and boarded the boat, then watched them pack the vessel to capacity with other passengers. We sank lower and lower in the water until it seemed I was standing under the sea, with water lapping at the boat's rim. If we rocked even slightly to one side, I thought we would keel over and sink.

The captain did exactly the opposite of what I wanted him to do: he took us into the open sea where the water was deep and dark and the shoreline seemed miles away. We chugged along there, dozens of people standing knee-deep in worry, watching the waves come within inches of over-taking the boat. After two hours we cut in to Beirut harbor. It took forever to reach the dock, but we finally arrived in late afternoon. No one had been lost. Not even my pant cuffs were wet. One of my cousins met me there and drove me to his home. I had not slept for nearly two days, and I fell into bed and slumbered soundly in one of the most dangerous cities in the world.

The next morning everything went as planned: I met the people from the radio station and gave them my tapes to air so they could keep their commitment to Pat. *How many people will meet the Lord because of these tapes?* I wondered. *What will the impact on eternity be? Lord, I pray it will be great.*

After our meeting I took the same half-sunk boat to the dock near Sidon, holding my breath most of the way. I arrived there in the early afternoon. But this time I was forbidden to enter the city.

"You need permission from the commander of the Israeli army to go into Sidon," they told me. "Go to his office in that village."

He pointed the way, and I obeyed and went to the village. As I looked at the line of people waiting to get permission, I realized it was Friday afternoon, and I would never make it to the border before 5:00 p.m. when the Sabbath began. Once the Sabbath was underway, Israel would shut down, and the Israeli border would close. My plane was scheduled to leave on Saturday morning from Israel to America. I couldn't afford to miss it.

"Lord, what am I doing in this line?" I said. "I'll never

make it back at this rate. They are interviewing each person individually."

The Lord said, "Go to the front and talk to the man in charge about your situation."

I stepped out and walked forward. The soldier in charge stiffened as I approached, but as I drew near he looked at me, and his eyes brightened with recognition. He softened his stance.

"How can I help you, Dr. Malki?" he said. He must have recognized me from television.

WHEN I HAD FINISHED PRAYING I TOLD THE DRIVER, "EXCUSE ME, I JUST MADE A PRIVATE TELEPHONE CALL."

"I need to get to the border before the Sabbath," I said.

"Wait here," he said, then went inside the gate. He returned moments later and opened the gate for me.

"This way," he said, and led me into the commander's office. A man of responsibility sat at a desk. He looked up as I walked in.

"This man has an urgent need to reach the border," said the soldier. The commander took my passport and gave me the permission I needed to enter Sidon. I thanked them both, rushed out, took a taxi to Sidon, and arrived at 3:00 p.m. I was making good time, but there was still a two-hour drive to the border.

"Driver," I said, "get me to the border, fast."

He looked at me as if I were crazy.

"It will be impossible to get you there before 5:00 p.m., even if I go the speed limit, which is impossible to do because of the military vehicles around here. The road is only two lanes, and if we get behind a military convoy we cannot pass them because it is against the law unless they stop and motion for you to pass."

"I need to get there," I said. "I believe we can do it."

He sighed.

"OK, I will take you—but if we get stopped, I will have to bring you back. There are no hotels over there."

"Very well," I said.

I got in the front seat, and within twenty minutes we found ourselves behind two military tanks going thirty-five miles per hour. The driver looked at me skeptically.

"We had better go back," he said. "Why should I go all the way behind these tanks? You will miss the deadline anyway."

I did not answer. Logic would not work in that situation. Instead I opened my mouth and prayed in the Spirit. I didn't know what else to do. When I had finished praying I told the driver, "Excuse me, I just made a private telephone call." I pointed to the tanks and said, "Stop!" At that moment, the tanks stopped and motioned for us to pass them. The driver didn't hesitate, though I could see the look of astonishment on his face. When we were safely ahead of them he looked at me sideways.

"What kind of work do you do?" he said.

"I am an ambassador."

"For what country?"

"Never mind. Step on it," I said.

We arrived at the Lebanese border at 4:55 p.m. The driver looked at his watch and shook his head in disbelief.

"I still cannot take you across this military zone," he said, but I had already gotten out of the car. One of the guards came closer and peered at me. His face broke into a smile.

"Oh, Dr. Malki. I watch you on TV," he said.

"Good," I said. "Listen, I have to get to the other side before they close the gate. I can't make it in time if I walk. Would you allow the driver to take me across?"

The guard looked at the cab driver.

"Go ahead and take Dr. Malki across," he said, waving him on.

By this time the driver was slack-jawed with amazement. I could see the question running all over his face: *Who is this passenger I picked up?*

I got in the car, and we drove across the no-man's-land and arrived at the Israeli border as the gate was ready to close. I paid the driver and rushed across into Israel, but virtually nobody was on the other side. I looked around. There was not a single taxi or bus. The Sabbath had begun. I was miles away from civilization, sweating and tired.

"Lord, how am I going to get a ride to a hotel?" I said, and then I thought of Jeff. I had no idea what had happened to him. Before I finished asking the Lord my question, a man appeared on the side of the road with a bag in his hand. I hailed him.

"I need to get to Tel Aviv. Can you help me?" I said.

In Arabic he told me he was the owner of a little convenience store that had just closed. He was waiting for his son to pick him up. In the meantime he took me to his shop, and I changed clothes. Then his son arrived—in a two-seat car. They didn't want to take me, but I begged them, and somehow we managed to squeeze in together. Half an hour later we were at the bus station, but I had none of the proper currency, so the old man reached into his pocket and gave me money for the bus.

Then he turned to his son.

"I want to ride with this man on the bus," he said. "I will come home later. Tell your mother to wait for me."

The son was somewhat surprised, but he agreed and drove off. His father rode with me on the bus, then helped me buy a ticket at the train station. I thanked him, paid him back in dollars for the ticket, and settled into my seat on the train. Then a man came by to sweep the area I was sitting in. I looked at him and realized I knew him, though I had not seen him in forty years.

"Elias Zenati," I said.

He looked up. "Who are you?" he said.

"I am Elias Malki," I said. "We played marbles together forty years ago. We were neighbors."

"I don't remember that, but aren't you the man on TV?" he said.

"Yes, but I was also your neighbor. Remember one day we were playing marbles together? I got mad at you, we had a fight, and I hit you, and you hit me."

"Oh, yes," he said. "Now I remember."

We fell into conversation, and he didn't appear to want to leave, so I asked him, "Well, what can I do for you?"

"I want to give my heart to Jesus," he said. After such a topsy-turvy twenty-four hours, I was only mildly surprised by his forthrightness. We prayed together, and he received

Jesus as his Lord and Savior. Then he moved me to first class.

I arrived in Tel Aviv and went to a hotel, still wondering what had happened to Jeff. I got my answer the next morning as I stood in line at the airport. Jeff was right in front of me.

"When did you get back?" he asked, looking a little bemused. His adventure had been cut short when he could not accompany me, and he had sat for two days and nights in a hotel in Israel. I began to tell him what I had been through, but just then the security people pulled him aside and quizzed him for a long time. They opened his luggage and poked through his personal items. By the time they had finished, he was thoroughly upset.

But when my turn came, they asked me two questions and waved me through without incident. Jeff was steamed.

"How come they let you go so easy?" he said when we were beyond them.

Now I was the one bemused, but I simply replied, "I don't know. It's just been one of those trips."

Chapter 12

PENETRATING THE DARKNESS

As THE TELEVISION program gained a wider audience, letters began pouring into our ministry with testimonies of miracles. I was in Haifa ministering when a pastor of a Baptist church asked me, "Have you ever met Abou Fouad? He is an Arab man who was healed of a cancerous tumor when he prayed with you while watching your program. The whole city knows about it."

"I have never heard of him," I said.

He gave me the man's telephone number, and I made an appointment to meet him in his home. My daughter Ruth and my cameraman accompanied me. When we got there he related his story.

"One morning I woke up and noticed there was a red circle

on my side," he said. "I showed it to my wife. We made an appointment with the doctor, and he admitted me into the hospital. I was there for forty-one days. I developed a malignant tumor the size of a small watermelon. Then they sent me home on a Friday and said I must return for surgery on Monday morning.

"On that Sunday afternoon, my son-in-law and I were sitting on the couch. We turned on the TV. Your program was on, and you began to encourage people to believe in God and to pray with you. You said that God was able to heal no matter what the problem or sickness, because He is the God of miracles. Then you looked at me and said, 'You, sitting on the couch. Get up and put your hand on the TV and your other hand on your stomach and pray this prayer.' I knew you were talking to me, but I looked at my son-in-law, and he didn't make a move. We did not believe like you believe, so I didn't want to get up and do this in front of him. I was afraid he would tell on me. Then again you said, 'You, sitting on the couch, get up!' I wanted to get up. I looked at my son-in-law, and he didn't say a word. Then you stood up and got very loud and said, 'You, come and put your hand on the TV!' My son-in-law said, 'He is talking to you! Get up.'

"I got up and put my hand on the TV, and as you began to pray I repeated the prayer. I had never prayed to God in that manner. I went to sleep that night. The next morning we got up and prepared to go to the hospital. As I was putting my clothes on, I noticed the tumor was gone! I was shocked. I called my wife, and she came and looked at my side. The tumor was gone.

"We wanted to be sure everything was OK, so we still went to the hospital. Three doctors and a professor were supposed to do the surgery on me, but from 9:00 a.m. to noon they examined me and were confused. I told them what happened. They discharged me and sent me home."

"I SAID TO MYSELF, *WHAT DO I HAVE TO LOSE? I AM GOING TO CALL JESUS THE SON OF GOD.*"

"Who healed you?" I asked.

"God," he said.

"In whose name?" I said,

"In the name of Jesus," he said.

"Would you like to accept Jesus as your Savior?" I asked.

"Yes," he said. He, his wife, and their four children knelt with Ruth and me, and the whole family received Jesus as their Savior. Later, I said, "Do you mind if we put this interview on TV?"

"No, it is the truth," he said, so we aired it.

Later I went to Nazareth, and a pastor there asked me, "Have you met Zaccheus? He was healed of heart trouble, asthma, and arthritis when he prayed with you on TV."

He gave me Zaccheus's telephone number, and my cameraman and I went to his home. Zaccheus was around sixty years old, a Jew born in Egypt who spoke Arabic. (There are more than two million Jews living in Israel who emigrated from Arab countries. Their culture and language is Arabic but they are Jews.) He welcomed me into his home with a hug.

"Zaccheus, tell me your story," I said, and he began:

"I have been suffering for many years with arthritis in my joints and knees. I could hardly walk without a cane. Breathing was difficult because I had bad asthma. My heart functions at only 70 percent. I am on disability. The government gives me money to live. My wife passed away. My three children are married, and I live alone.

HE PRAYED TO GOD IN THE NAME OF JESUS, THE SON OF GOD, TO HEAL HER AND GIVE THEM CHILDREN. THIRTY DAYS LATER SHE CONCEIVED.

"I was watching your program. I understood everything you said. I watched you for six months, but I never called Jesus the Son of God like you always say. Every time I watched you, I said I would not listen to you again. But every time your program was on I watched anyway. A few months ago when I turned the TV on to watch you, my asthma was so bad I could barely breathe. My heart was skipping beats, and I was in great pain. I said to myself, *What do I have to lose? I am going to call Jesus the Son of God.*

"I responded to your invitation to touch the TV and put my other hand on my body. As you began to pray, for the first time in my life I called Jesus the Son of the living

God. I asked Him to heal me. I felt a jolt of electricity go from my head down to my toes. It shook me. I took a deep breath, and my lungs felt normal. I felt so good! My heart felt healthy. I walked back to my chair without my cane. You offered a Bible to whoever wanted it, but I wanted one so badly that I didn't want to wait. I took public transportation the next morning all the way to Nazareth and bought a Bible. I have been reading it now for months. Jesus is my Messiah."

Pat Robertson aired that interview many times on CBN.

On another occasion I was driving through Haifa on Mt. Carmel with my cameraman when we stopped at a roadside shop to buy a straw basket for my daughter Ruth. The store owner saw us come in and ran up to me with great excitement.

"Oh, you got my aunt's letter, and you are coming to visit with her!" he said.

"What do you mean?" I said. He grabbed me by the arm and took me to the back of the store, where he lived. His mother and aunt were there.

"Oh, you got my letter, and you came to see me," said his aunt. "I don't believe in God. So I wrote you a letter and said, 'If this busy man can accept my invitation and come to see me, I will believe in God.'"

Bewildered, I played along.

"Here I am. I came," I said. I prayed with her, and she received Christ. I prayed with the mother also. The young man who owned the store was smoking a cigarette and watching us.

"Put the cigarette down and pray with me," I said, and he prayed the sinner's prayer, too. When we got back in the car I marveled at how my apparent whim to stop and buy a basket was actually a divine appointment. I even ended up getting three straw baskets for free.

Later, I spoke at an open-air meeting in upper Galilee where the message I preached in English was interpreted into Arabic, Hebrew, and Spanish. I spoke for thirty minutes, and the sermon took two hours. Many people came to Christ. After the service, a man who stood six feet six or so approached me with his young wife and a baby.

"I have a story to tell you," he said.

He and his wife had been married for eight years, but she was barren. In his religion, he was allowed to marry more than one wife or to divorce his wife and marry another woman, if he chose. He didn't want to divorce his wife because he loved her, and he couldn't afford to marry another woman and support two wives. But he desperately wanted children. One day, he turned on the TV and saw the *Good News* program. At my invitation, he and his wife put their hands on the TV and on his wife's stomach. He prayed to God in the name of Jesus, the Son of God, to heal her and give them children. Thirty days later she conceived.

"We have a son now," he said. "Here he is. We called him, 'Gift of God.'"

He handed me the boy who was two years old.

"Do you want to receive Jesus as your Savior?" I asked the man.

"Yes, I do," he said, and I prayed with him and his wife.

Around that time another viewer, an Arab Iraqi Jew, discovered she had lumps in her breast that were getting larger. The doctor found they were all malignant and recommended surgery as soon as possible, but a friend suggested they watch the *Good News* program and pray with me.

"I watched you one time, two times, three times," this woman told me the day I visited her in her home. "Faith started coming to me when I heard the testimonies, and I believed. One Friday night when the program was on, I put one hand on the TV and put the other hand on my body, and for the first time I prayed in the name of Jesus the Son of God. A week or so went by, and I went back to the doctor. There were no more lumps. I was healed."

I HAD GONE FROM PASTORING A
CHURCH IN BEIRUT WHERE WE
COUNTED THE CONVERTS AND MIRACLES
IN THE DOZENS, TO PREACHING THE
GOSPEL TO MILLIONS EVERY WEEK.

"Who healed you?" I asked. It was my favorite question to ask such people.

"God," she said.

"In whose name?" I asked.

"In the name of Jesus," she said.

Then her daughter chimed in with her own story. "A month after my mother was healed, I felt lumps in my breast. The doctor confirmed that they were malignant. Right away I knew what to do. When your program came on, I put my hand on the TV and prayed the prayer of faith, calling Jesus the Son of God. I was healed just like my mother."

"Do you mind if I put these interviews on TV?" I asked.

"No, we don't mind," they said. While I continued interviewing the daughter, the Lord spoke to my spirit and said, "Pray for this young lady, and I will baptize her in the Holy Spirit."

"Turn off the camera," I told my cameraman. I turned back to the daughter. "May I pray for you now?"

"Yes," she said, and as soon as I laid my hands on her head she began to speak in tongues and magnify the Lord in languages she had never learned.

Word of these signs and wonders spread all over the Middle East, and thousands of letters poured into the Good News office in Cyprus. I had gone from pastoring a church in Beirut where we counted the converts and miracles in the dozens, to preaching the gospel to millions every week.

⟶

But being a television personality didn't shield me from the persecution that Christians so commonly experience in the Middle East. In January 1985, I traveled to Egypt with my director, David, and my cameraman, Greg. We had a full schedule of interviews to record and air on the *Good News* program. We arrived at the passport desk in Cairo at 9:00 p.m., expecting to sail through, but they took our passports and were gone for half an hour. They brought back David's and Greg's passports, but not mine.

"You may leave," they said to them, "but Mr. Malki, you must stay behind."

"Don't leave," I told David and Greg, sensing the situation might turn unfavorable. It was getting later, and we waited again, not knowing why. Then a man came from the passport authorities.

"Where are your belongings?" he said.

"Here," I said. I had my garment bag and my briefcase. It was full of testimonies from the *Good News* program.

"Follow me," he said, then stopped and looked at David and Greg.

"You can leave," he said, but David and Greg said, "No. We will stay with Dr. Malki."

They waited in the lobby for me. I followed the passport official, who took me into a room and sat me before three other men whose heads were covered. All I could see were their eyes, noses, and mouths. They began to interrogate me. I immediately prayed that they would not search my luggage and find the testimonies, which would have meant trouble for me.

"What do you do?" they asked.

"I am a preacher of the gospel," I said.

"Where is your church?"

"I travel all over the world. I have a traveling ministry."

"To whom do you preach?"

"To whoever will listen."

"No. You are converting Muslims."

"You mean I have the power to convert Muslims?" I said.

"Shut up!" one of them said.

I became quiet. I felt as if my briefcase had a bull's-eye target on it. If they opened it and found the stack of stories from Arab viewers of the *Good News* program, they might take their anger out on me.

The questioning began again and continued for an hour. Not once did they even glance at my luggage. Finally they said, "You are not allowed to come to this country any more. You are not welcome here."

"Why?" I asked.

"You have to discuss that with the authorities in Cairo. Bring your belongings and follow this man."

I took my garment bag and briefcase and followed another man to a room ten feet long and four feet wide. It contained only a chair and, inexplicably, a cat with three or four kittens. I did not like cats, and I did not like that room.

"You stay here until the morning," he said. "Your flight will leave at 5:00 a.m., and you must be on it."

"I am an American," I said. "I don't need to stay here. I have a reservation at the Hilton. I have to go. My colleagues are waiting for me."

"Would you pay for a room at the airport tonight, if we let you?" he asked.

"Yes," I said. He left the room and then came back.

"Follow me," he said.

David and Greg were still waiting for me in the hallway. We paid for a hotel room at the airport, though it was nothing more than a bare room with three beds and a host of roaches. They sent a policeman to guard me for the next four hours before my plane left. David, Greg, and

I were tired, but we hoped to brush our teeth, for which we needed bottled water. I asked the guard, whose name was Muhammad, to buy us bottled water. I gave him five dollars, equal to a day's wages.

"I am not supposed to leave you, sir," he said.

"Where am I going to run off to?" I said. "I don't have a passport."

He considered this, then walked off, and returned with two bottles of water.

"These people were very mean to you," he said. I just smiled. Then the Lord said, "Tell him about Me." As I opened my mouth, the Lord opened his heart, and I shared the gospel with him. I prayed with him, and he received Jesus as his Savior. David took a picture of him and me. He was smiling from ear to ear. He gave me his address, and later I sent him a copy of the picture.

Five o'clock in the morning came, and we had not slept. A new guard told us to follow him, and when we arrived at the gate to board the plane, he told David and Greg to go through a different door. Then a government official held my passport in his hand and led me another way.

"You can have your passport after you pay me a tip," he said.

"What do you mean *a tip*?" I said.

"A tip for giving you the passport," he said. "Enough to buy my cigarettes for a day."

I waited a few moments, resisting the bribe. He held onto my passport and would not budge. Finally I reached into my pocket and gave him a few dollars. He handed over my passport and took me to a bus. I was the only passenger, except for the new guard.

"Why did you people do this to me?" I asked him.

"We didn't do it," he said. "Your own people delivered you to us."

I didn't know what he meant, but it was possible that, because of my Charismatic teaching, some people in the religious community had given information that got me onto a blacklist.

I boarded the plane with David and Greg, and that was the last time I was physically in Egypt. But in a way I have been in that country ever since my radio program began. The *Good News* program aired there three times a week from 1982 to 1994, and since 1996 the *Good News* program airs four times a day through satellite television, and I am now off the blacklist.

~ᴄ᭫ Chapter 13 ᭫ᴄ~

DIVINE DIRECTION

A s the *Good News* program flourished, I threw myself into television ministry, knowing that God had opened a window of opportunity to reach the Arab world like never before. By 1992 I felt another burden: to establish a training center for people who were getting saved through the program. The idea was to train them for three months and send them back to their countries where they could be ministers of the gospel right where they lived. But we had to find a place for a Christian training institute where it would be safe from attack. As I was praying, the Holy Spirit said, "Go to Cyprus." That island would again play a pivotal part in bringing the gospel to the Arab world.

I flew there with my English friends Mervyn and Edna Tilley. Mervyn is the district superintendent of Elim Pentecostal Churches in the London metropolitan area. We spent days on Cyprus looking for a place to house the training center, but the moment we told people what we intended to use it for, they refused to lease to us. In their minds I was a protestor, a Protestant, an evangelical. I was, they believed, against the historical church to which they belonged.

I began to wonder if I had heard the Lord correctly, but on the last day someone told us to visit the bishop of the city of Limassol on the southern part of the island.

HERE I WAS, AN EVANGELICAL PROTESTANT—A HERETIC IN THE EYES OF THE ORTHODOX CHURCH, AND YET GOD GAVE US FAVOR WITH THE BISHOP.

"He is cooperative and open-minded, and he has a building in the mountains," this person promised, so I called and made an appointment to meet the bishop that afternoon. We drove an hour to Limassol and met him, and I told him about my background, my television show, and what I wanted to do with a training center.

"Do these Arab people really get converted?" he asked, incredulous.

"I don't convert them. God converts them through the Word," I said. "I have letters to prove it."

He pondered my words for a moment, then said, "You are welcome to see the place up in the mountains. It is half an hour drive from here."

He rang a bell, and his driver entered the room.

"Take them to the property in the mountains," he said, and soon we were being whisked there in a black Mercedes limousine.

It was January; the weather was quite cold and the snow on the mountain was just beginning to melt. The place we were visiting used to be a sanitarium for tuberculosis patients who recuperated in the fresh mountain air. The man who had owned it donated the property to the Orthodox church before he died.

The Tilleys and I walked the property, and I knew it would be perfect for us. We came back down the mountain and met with the bishop again.

"We most certainly could use the facility," I said.

He replied, "We do use it in July and August for summer camp for our children, but the rest of the year you are welcome to it."

I kept his gaze, prepared now to talk finances.

"How much rent will you require?" I asked.

"Are those people who watch your program really being converted?" he said.

"Yes," I said. "God loves them. Jesus died for everybody. At one time this island did not believe in Jesus, and it took one supernatural miracle through Paul and Barnabas to convince the governor of the island to become a Christian. Then the whole island became Christian. That is why you are bishop now."

He smiled at me.

"Then the least I can do is to give you the property for no rent."

I could barely speak. Here I was, an evangelical Protestant—a heretic in the eyes of the Orthodox church, and yet God gave us favor with the bishop.

We opened Mego Christian Center in 1993 with eight Arab students. Our staff consisted of an Arab teacher from Jordan, a dean from Texas who had lived in the Middle East before, a business manager and his wife from England, a custodian and his wife from the United States, and a Greek cook and his wife.

IT WAS THE MOST AWESOME BEGINNING I COULD HAVE IMAGINED— AND I DIDN'T EVEN PLAN IT.

Our first obstacle was getting all our students into Cyprus. They could not enter the island without an official invitation from a nonprofit organization sponsoring their stay. I had favor with the bishop of Limassol, and he extended an invitation to six of the students who came from one Arab country. But the other two arrived at the airport in Larnaca, Cyprus, without an invitation. The immigration officials stopped them and would not allow them to enter the country. I pleaded with them to give them visas, but they refused.

"Then I must meet with the head of the immigration," I demanded.

They took me to the man's office, and the minute I stepped in his eyes fell on the bolo tie I was wearing. It bore an American silver dollar. I had never worn bolo ties before, but the previous month I had preached in Knoxville, Tennessee, and a man came up to me after the service wearing a bolo tie. He took it from his neck and handed it to me.

"Take this and wear it," he had said. "The day will come when you will need it!"

I started wearing it with sport shirts because Donna liked the way it looked. Now the head of the immigration couldn't take his eyes off of it.

"I like that tie," he said. "I collect them."

"How many do you have?" I asked.

"I have many bolo ties at home," he said.

"I would like to see them," I said.

"OK," he said. "I will be glad to show you."

He gave me his home phone number, and I told him I would come by to see his collection. Then he looked at me and said, "This time we will let you bring those two young men in the country, but next time you have to have an invitation."

With his approval, the two young men sailed through, and we were on our way to the training center.

To my knowledge, in all the Middle East there was no such training center designed for Arab people only. After a celebratory opening session, which was attended by friends and supporters from several continents, I was on the first floor balcony talking to the Greek cook and his wife, who was also an interpreter. She was a devoted Christian and was baptized in the Holy Spirit, but her husband had only recently received Jesus Christ. I wanted to be sure he had the baptism of the Holy Spirit, too.

His wife was holding a Greek Bible, so I opened it and happened to put my finger on Acts 2, which I didn't know because I do not read Greek. "Read this to your husband," I said. "Let him understand it in Greek." She read it aloud, and through her interpretation I explained the importance of the baptism of the Holy Spirit to him. I didn't know that above me on the second floor balcony the dean of the center and one of our students were listening to our conversation. All of a sudden I heard shouting, scuffling, and unidentifiable noises coming from above us. I left the cook and his wife and rushed to the second floor. There I saw that the power of God had come upon the student, and Jesus had baptized him in the Holy Spirit. Nobody had put a hand on him, but now he was speaking in tongues so loudly that his voice filled the area.

"Let's bring the others in," I said to the dean, and we brought the other seven students into a nearby room, and they were all baptized in the Holy Spirit as well. It was the most awesome beginning I could have imagined—and I didn't even plan it. Our visitors from England and America were amazed.

A new group of students arrived at the center every three months, and my staff and I soon discovered that most of them knew nothing about Jesus except what they heard on the *Good News* program. One young man had picked up a teaching from missionaries in his home country who did not believe in the baptism of the Holy Spirit. He had many questions, and after discussing it with the dean, he concluded that the experience was not for today.

But the next morning he went to the dean and said, "I had a dream last night. I was sitting at a table with you and two other brothers. In front of each of us was a glass. Your glass was full, and the other two were full, but mine was empty. A voice spoke to me in my dream and said, 'You need to be filled with the Holy Spirit. You are empty.' Will you please pray for me?"

The dean laid hands on him, and he fell under the power and spoke in tongues. He became a full-time minister in Morocco.

"NOW WE KNOW YOUR GOD IS GOD. WE WANT TO KNOW THIS GOD, AND WE WANT HIM TO BE OUR GOD."

Another young man came after receiving a five-star secular education. He had watched me on television and received healing for his body. He had also accepted Christ. He came to the school when I happened to be visiting, and we prayed for him. He fell to the floor and began to behave strangely, and we had to cast three demons out of him. He later married a beautiful young woman and went into full-time ministry.

Our training center met in that mountain facility for six years, and then a new bishop took the place of the one I had known. He asked me to leave and turn over the property to him. I was reminded of the story in the Bible of Joseph, when there arose a pharaoh that did not know Joseph. The new bishop would not meet with me, and he didn't give us much time to find another place. I had a legal right to stay, because of the agreement I had signed with the previous bishop, but we began looking for another place. We encountered the same resistance as before, and I prayed hard about the subject. It took two years, but finally we found a facility not two miles from the bishop's property, and it worked out to be a much better arrangement for the school than the first property had been.

As our Good News office received more stories of people whose lives were radically changed through the television program, I was amazed by the commitment of Arab people whose Christian faith put them at risk of death. One boy living in northern Jordan was the only child of extremely wealthy parents who were quite religious but were not Christians. He watched my program secretly because he was a minor, and his parents would not have approved. One day he responded to the invitation to receive Jesus as his personal Savior, a fact he kept strictly under wraps.

But when he turned eighteen, he decided to tell his parents the truth.

"I have been watching the *Good News* program on television," he told them. "I heard the gospel. I prayed and received Jesus Christ as my Lord and Savior. I am now a Christian."

His parents were stunned, but they kept quiet and the boy was relieved that they were not as angry as he had anticipated.

Two weeks later the parents sat him down for a talk.

"Because you backslid from our faith, you deserved to die," his father said. "We love you, but we had to do what we felt was right according to our faith. We didn't want to kill you in a way the public would know about it, so we decided to poison your food. We were hoping this would take care of the matter. We poisoned your food, but it didn't hurt you. We increased the amount of poison a second time, and it still did not hurt you. We could hardly believe it. We increased the poison a third time, and yet you are still alive. Now we know your God is God. We want to know this God, and we want Him to be our God."

The young man introduced them to the *Good News* program. The father and mother received the Lord as their personal Savior.

On another occasion I was visiting the city of Akko in Israel when I heard my name: "Dr. Malki! Dr. Malki!" I turned to see a woman flagging me down.

"You must go see my brother in the village of Makkar," she said. "My nephew was healed."

I took her brother's phone number and made an appointment to go see him. When I got there with my cameraman, the people from the village lined the street and were waving palm branches and saying, "Welcome, Dr. Malki." The house was bursting with people. The father hugged me and invited me in. We set up our camera to record his story for our program.

"My wife and I have two girls, and I love them," he said. "But you know that in the Middle Eastern culture it is important to have a male child. So I kept praying for a boy. Two years ago my wife had a boy, but when he was born he had brain damage. He could not lift his arms or legs, nor focus his eyes. He could neither speak nor hear. Someone told me to watch the *Good News* program. They said God was using that program to heal people.

THE *GOOD NEWS* PROGRAM HAD REACHED FARTHER THAN I HAD EVER DREAMED.

"I watched one day, and from the beginning to the end I grabbed the TV set and asked God to heal my son. I was weeping. My wife was sitting on the couch with my son. She was weeping, too. When the program was over I turned around to look at my son. For the first time in his life he smiled and reached his hands to me. His eyes were focused. He moved his legs. I grabbed him and hugged him. Ever since then he has been normal. He walks, and he talks, and he hears!"

He put the boy on the floor and showed me how he could walk. I grabbed the boy in my arms and thanked God. The Lord spoke to my heart, "Tell these people about Me." I preached to all the people there in that house, and every person prayed the sinner's prayer.

I went to another home where the young leader of a secular nightclub band had been saved and liberated from his addictions to drugs, alcohol, and cigarettes. As we ate the feast his mother prepared for us, the young man's father told me about their youngest son.

178

"Your program comes on the same time that his favorite program comes on, so we always conflict about which program we will watch," the father said. "One day he walked in, and I was watching the *Good News* program. He reached for the dial, but you said, 'Young man, don't turn the channel! God is going to heal your eyes. Sit down and listen!' It scared him, so he sat down and listened. You called him to put his hand on the TV and pray with you. He put one hand on the TV and the other hand on his eyes and prayed with you. Minutes later he looked at me in shock. He said, 'Dad, I don't need these glasses anymore. I can see everything clearly!'"

Right then, the father handed me the boy's glasses across the table.

"Do you mind putting these on television so that the whole world will know about this?" he asked me. I did just as he asked, and our viewers saw again the power of God to heal.

The *Good News* program had reached farther than I had ever dreamed. Even the ambassador of Israel to the United States told me he watched it. But in spite of the historic results we were witnessing, a change in leadership at the broadcast company with whom we partnered meant a sudden lack of support from the people who made the decisions. In 1994 we parted ways with our longtime business partner, and the *Good News* program went off the air.

I was confused and angry. I had pioneered outreach to the Middle East; my program had aired three times a day for twelve years. I knew that the enemy did not like what God was accomplishing through the program, and I was certain that Satan had won a victory by disguising himself as an angel of light and deceiving good people into making a bad decision. But soon enough I would understand the truth of the Bible verse that says, "And we know that all things work together for good to them that love God, to them who are the called according to his purpose" (Rom. 8:28). Like Joseph, I would soon say that what had been meant for evil, God used for good.

~e? Chapter 14 ??

AN OPEN DOOR

OOD NEWS WAS off the air, and I felt wounded, unable to understand why God had let the program disappear from the airwaves. I was frustrated with the situation and with the men who had made it happen, but beneath all my emotions, I knew God had a purpose in it. Then God opened up an unexpected door and enabled me to strike up a friendship with a public figure I hadn't met up until then: Yasser Arafat.

When I was a missionary in Lebanon, our church had been only three miles from Arafat's headquarters in West Beirut. I had never had reason to meet him, though many Americans met with him, and some of them, reportedly, even prayed with him. But in 1994 while watching television, I saw President Bill Clinton and the prime minister of Israel, Yitzhak Rabin, shake hands with Arafat to show the world they agreed to the Oslo accord, which gave the West Bank to the Palestinians. Something within me said, "You need to meet Yasser Arafat and negotiate with him to build a television station in the West Bank."

I immediately began to inquire about how I might contact Arafat. A week after I had received the word from the Lord, I attended a missionary conference in St. Louis, Missouri. The evangelist speaker, Reverend Jim Maloney, was calling people forward and prophesying to them. The meeting was almost finished when he looked at me where I sat in the back.

"Aren't you Elias Malki?" he said. "Please come forward. The Lord has a word for you."

I went forward, and he prophesied that I would meet Yasser Arafat and would lay hands on him, pray for him, and he would be healed. He said I would have favor with Arafat and that he would help me accomplish what was in my heart. Jim had no prior knowledge of my desire to meet Mr. Arafat.

When I arrived home, my son Tim went to work to set up a meeting with Arafat. Tim had worked in the Middle East for several years and had an expertise in diplomacy. He found out that Arafat was in Tunis, North Africa. Tim and our general manager, Bill Finley, went to meet with his organization to schedule a meeting between Arafat and myself. We learned that other Christian leaders had met with him to secure their own licenses for television stations in the West Bank, but to my knowledge none of them received a license.

When Tim came back, he gave me the date Arafat and I were to meet. I took my board members with me—Claud Bowers of SuperChannel 55 in Orlando, Florida; Ben Frizzel from Frizzel Construction Company in Tennessee; Bud Keilani from Detroit; and Bill Finley. We landed at the airport in Tunis, drove to the Hilton Hotel, and made contact with one of Arafat's aides by telephone. Our appointment was for 4:00 p.m. that day.

"Your meeting has been postponed," the aide told me. "It will be tonight, but we don't know what time."

I alerted my board members to wait in their rooms and be ready within ten minutes of hearing from me. Arafat's aide met with me at the hotel and took detailed information about every person who would be meeting with his boss. Then he left, and we waited and waited. Finally, my telephone rang at 10:00 p.m.

IN THE NAME OF JESUS, I PRAYED FOR HIS HEALING, FOR WISDOM, AND FOR PEACE WITH THE NEW OSLO AGREEMENT.

"Be in the lobby in ten minutes," said the messenger. "There will be two cars to pick you up."

We didn't know where we were going, but we got into the cars and rode through the narrow streets of Tunis. Suddenly we stopped.

"Get out," the driver said.

We complied and found ourselves before a door guarded

by two armed militia men. They opened the door and took us through one hall after another. Finally we came to a room where they seated us. We waited for a few moments, and then Mr. Arafat walked in. He and I greeted one another the Middle Eastern way, with a kiss on the cheek.

After introducing my board members to him, I gave him a gift, which is the custom in the Middle East. The gift was a pair of dove pins that said, "Born again," one in Arabic and one in English. My wife, Donna, thought it would be symbolic of his determination and perseverance for the cause he believed in, and that because of his work, a nation called *Palestine* was "born again." He took the pins and was so thrilled that he laughed for a long time. Then he gave me a beautiful mother-of-pearl box handmade in Bethlehem. My board members exchanged gifts with him also, and for the next hour we shared with him our reason for being there. At the end of our time I told him, "We would like to pray for you, for whatever your need is. Would you like us to do that?"

"Yes," he said, so I laid my hand on him and the rest of the board members came close. In the name of Jesus, I prayed for his healing, for wisdom, and for peace with the new Oslo agreement. Before we left, he agreed to give us the permit for the TV station. He told us we needed to meet with his minister of communication the next day, and so we did, spending many hours hammering out a principal agreement.

A few months later, Arafat and his cabinet moved into the West Bank, and they met with Tim and me. The contract was drawn, and the license was issued to build a high power station in the West Bank. It would be a secular station that carried Christian programming as well. It would cost five million dollars to build the station—a staggering amount. We tried to raise the funds, but we had no practical way of bringing it in so fast. Other ministries had the money but not the license. We had the license but not the money. In the end, we did not raise the money and did not get the station.

〜⸺

But God was doing something through the relationship between Arafat and myself. God gave me favor with him, and I met with him three other times to renew our agreement for the license while we tried to raise the funds. The third meeting was in Gaza, which was at peace in those days. Jim Maloney and a pastor friend, Jerry Skinner, accompanied me to Tel Aviv. The day before our meeting I felt we should have lunch with a couple who had been touched by the *Good News* program. I asked Jim and Jerry if they would like to have lunch at the house of Simon the Tanner. The couple I wanted to have lunch with were the caretakers of the biblical site. The husband had been in a coma in 1991, and the doctors had given up on him. They had told his wife to prepare for his funeral, but she told the doctor she believed in Jesus Christ. That evening she had watched the *Good News* program and prayed with me for her husband's healing.

The next morning she received a call from the hospital: her husband had come out of the coma and was ready to go home.

Since then we had become good friends, so Jim, Jerry, and I drove about an hour to their home. I didn't give them any warning, which was unusual for me. When I rang the bell, the husband opened the door and welcomed us in.

"We want to have lunch with you, but we don't want you to pay for it," I said. "Could you come with me to buy some groceries?"

He agreed and went with me while Jim and Jerry stayed at the house. At the market we bought cheese, bread, vegetables, and fruit. But when we returned to the house, a beautiful table with a hot meal had already been spread out for us. I looked at his wife in amazement.

"When did you prepare that?" I asked.

THE MISSING COIN WAS THE FIVE PIASTERS—THE VERY COIN I HAD BROUGHT FROM AMERICA TO GIVE HIM.

"Last night, the Lord told me the man of God would be here tomorrow, and I should prepare a good meal for him," she said. "The Lord said the man would invite himself and would pray for my chest, and I would be healed. I don't know why my husband took you to the store. The food was ready."

I translated the story for Jim and Jerry, and they were as surprised and gratified as I was. We ate the delicious meal she had prepared, and after lunch we prayed for her, and she was healed.

Later that afternoon I tried to call Arafat's contact to let him know we were ready to meet with him at 6:00 p.m. as planned, but I kept making a mistake when dialing, and I didn't get through.

"We'll go to the border on faith and see if Arafat's contact is there," I said, and when we arrived at the border, he was there. We climbed into his armed Jeep.

"Mr. Arafat had a bad day today," he said. "One of his best friends passed away. He canceled all his meetings for today, even yours. But he knew you were already here, and he could not get in touch with you to let you know. He said he will meet with you at ten o'clock tonight because you came such a long way. But he is tired and won't spend a lot of time."

I realized that if I had dialed correctly, the aide would have canceled the meeting.

That night we met with Arafat, and as usual we exchanged gifts. Before I had left home, I had thought much about what kind of gift to take this time. I collect coins, and I had a number of old Palestinian coins that dated to the time when Palestine was under British rule. The coins were precious to me and were collectors' items. I told Donna what I intended to do, and Tim was standing there, too.

"What a cheap gift," they both told me. "You don't want to give him a coin."

I respected their opinions, but something deep inside me said, "That's what he needs. Take it and give it to him." Half an hour before I left for the airport, I took the coin to a shop and had a plastic cover put over it to protect it. Then I put the coin in my wallet.

When Mr. Arafat came into the room that night looking tired, I pulled out the coin and handed it to him.

"This is something very precious to me," I said. "I have

kept it for fifty-two years. For some reason, I felt I should give it to you. I hope you enjoy it."

He looked at the coin, and the frown on his face turned into a beaming smile. He laid the coin on his desk, then stood up, reached into his pocket, and pulled out a napkin. He unwrapped it and laid a coin from it on the desk. Then he reached into another pocket and pulled out another coin, and then another and another. In all he pulled six coins from his pockets. Three were Roman coins that dated back two thousand years. The other three were Palestinian coins that dated back fifty years. The Palestinian coins were a series of ten piasters, two piasters, and one piaster. The missing coin was the five piasters—the very coin I had brought from America to give him. My gift completed his collection.

Mr. Arafat could not believe his eyes. Everyone, including his usually somber aides, laughed heartily.

"I have been looking for this for many, many years," Arafat said.

We had a good conversation after that and discussed our business. Then they drove us to the border, and we drove back to the hotel. From that day on Mr. Arafat never called me by my name as he had before; instead he called me the "holy man of God."

I met with him again a few months later, but by then the situation in the West Bank had gotten violent. The area became dangerous, and, aside from our lack of finances, we were reluctant to proceed with the television station since it would be in a war zone and could easily be bombed. But I still knew that God was not finished with me in television ministry.

In November 1995, God sent a confirmation. I was taking a group of eighteen Americans from the Holy Land to London. A woman who supported my ministry and had spent many years in the Holy Land saw me on the airplane.

ON JUNE 1, 1996, FOR THE FIRST TIME IN THE HISTORY OF THE CHURCH, THE GOSPEL WENT FORTH IN ARABIC ON SATELLITE TELEVISION, COVERING SEVENTY-SEVEN NATIONS EVERY FRIDAY.

"I have been looking for you for over a year," she said. "I have a word for you from the Lord. I feel I should give it to you right now."

"Go ahead," I said.

She began to speak in another language in the Spirit, and everybody, including the strangers sitting next to me, listened. Then she interpreted what she had said:

> You already know this—God shut a door for you. It was not man, but God, because you were operating on too small of a level. The Holy Ghost says He is releasing a mantle over you to take the Word of the Lord into the satellite realm. Because you are a man that will not give up, and because of the years you have sown faithfully into the harvest, yea, I will call forth a people of substance to give the funds to this satellite television. You have been sowing in a small area in the airwaves, but it has been enlarged

to include the footprints of the Middle East, Europe, North Africa, and Asia. According to your faith it shall be enlarged—enlarged! Your satellite TV shall be in the Arabic language, and it shall go beyond the border. For I am the God that goes beyond the border. I shall not be stopped on the ground. I am lifting up your gift through the airwaves to the nations, up from the ground, up to the satellite, and beaming back down. It shall bypass all ideologies, and I say that this mantle is yours. I have offered this to others, and they have not had the strength or endurance or patience to accept it. But in you I have found a servant who will break through into this realm; who will not let go of Me until you have it, says God. This is only a confirmation of what you know in your spirit, that God has given you the authority to enlarge, up, up, up beyond men's political maneuverings, whether they be believers or the unbelievers.

The words rang true to me. A year before, God had spoken to me that I would be the first man to go on satellite television and preach the gospel in Arabic. I didn't know how to do it or who to call, but now he was confirming His promise to me publicly.

"Thank you for being faithful to the Lord by bringing me this word," I said to the woman, and I knew without a doubt that soon the door would open.

In February 1996 the general manager of a television station in El Paso, Texas, Grace Rendall, called and said the Lord had told her I should meet an Englishman named Chris Dandridge, a satellite broker who had a half-hour airtime slot available. The satellite channel was secular, but this woman told Chris he needed to make the slot available to me. Chris came all the way to southern California to meet with me, and I signed a contract to purchase the time.

On June 1, 1996, for the first time in the history of the church, the gospel went forth in Arabic on satellite television, covering seventy-seven nations every Friday night at 7:00 p.m., Middle East time. By faith, I had signed a contract to pay $1,500 every week, a dizzying amount for me, but I knew God wanted me on the air. I had been silent for almost two years, but God was fulfilling what He had put in my heart.

I SHOOK THE MAN'S HAND, BUT IN THE BACK OF MY MIND I COULD ALMOST HEAR THE CRIES OF THE PEOPLE WHO WERE SLAUGHTERED THAT DAY SO LONG AGO.

Letters again poured into our office in Cyprus, and not just from Arab countries, but now from Europe and North Africa as well. A Moroccan woman living in the Ukraine wrote to share her heartbreaking but victorious story.

"I came to the Ukraine because my brother and his wife promised to help me finish my college, but they had other motives," she related. "They wanted a babysitter. They never sent me to college. I couldn't go back home because I didn't have the money.

"I was so depressed I made up my mind to kill myself. When I was ready to hang myself in my room, something told me to turn the TV on. It was very strange. When I turned the TV on the *Good News* program was on. You said, 'There is a young woman watching. You are twenty-two years old. You are very depressed, and you are about to kill yourself. You just turned the TV on. Don't take your life. It is wrong. You should listen. I have news for you. Jesus died for you on the cross. He loves you, and He wants to give you joy, peace, and forgiveness. Why don't you put your hand on the TV and pray this prayer?'

"I knew you were talking to me. I put my hand on the TV and prayed to God using the name of Jesus, the Son of God. Something happened in me. I felt something leave me, and peace and joy filled my soul and mind. That is why I am so happy, but I don't know how to pray and what to say. So, please send me the Bible that you have offered that I might be able to understand more about Jesus."

Letters like that thrilled our hearts, but after being on the air for a year, God had another unexpected lesson for me to learn. I went to London to sign a contract for another year. Chris Dandridge met me at the Heathrow Park Hotel, and there he introduced me to a gentleman whom he referred to as a "Kurdish leader in exile." Of course, the Kurds were well-known to me. Kurds had been responsible for the massacre in Karadesh where my grandfather and uncle were martyred. I shook the man's hand, but in the back of my mind I could almost hear the cries of the people who were slaughtered that day so long ago. Their memory, and the memory of my grandfather, had never left me.

"This man has just leased a twenty-four-hour satellite channel, and he wants to broadcast programs for the Kurdish people who live in Syria, Iraq, Iran, and Turkey," Chris said as we sat down for a meal. I recalled that the borders of those four nations, where the Kurds live, is known as Kurdistan, though it is not an actual nation. The Kurds have tried to establish a nation for years, but those nations refuse to cede any land.

"He wants to unite Kurds through his satellite network," Chris continued, "but he needs a satellite uplink, which can only be licensed by the government of the country from where you uplink. No Middle Eastern or European country will give him a license for fear of reprisal from those four nations."

Chris turned to me.

"I have been unable to help this gentleman get an uplink. Would you pray that I will be able to help him?" he asked.

"I will be happy to pray," I said, "but remember I have to pray in the name of Jesus, and this gentleman is not a Christian."

They both agreed that I could pray however I wished to pray, and we bowed our heads and I prayed that God would help Chris find an uplink for this Kurdish man. Then we went our separate ways.

After our meeting my mind went back to the summer of 1965 when I was a missionary in Beirut and my father had visited us from California. He had asked me to take him to Karadesh during his stay, so we loaded our green Mercury sedan, and Donna, the kids, and I began our thousand-mile journey to Turkey.

We arrived there in the morning and found our way to the village where my grandfather and his family had been missionaries. Things were completely different than when my father had last been there at age twenty—the day he fled the jihad. He was now sixty-eight. I stopped the car in the center of town, and Dad opened the car door and looked around. Then, with great excitement, he pointed to a house.

"That was our house," he said. Then he began to shake with emotion.

"Dad, it's OK. Come take a seat in the car," I said. To calm him, I turned on the car radio, and a famous Lebanese country singer was singing a popular Lebanese song about people who leave their country and return after a long time. The lyrics were something like this:

> After a long absence we came home
> looking for the folks.
> We found the house,
> but the folks are gone.

"Did you put that cassette tape in the car just for me?" Dad asked me.

"No," I replied, "it is not a cassette. I just turned the radio on."

Tears streamed down his face as he listened to the song, and the rest of us began to cry, too. It was as if we were having a long-awaited memorial for my grandfather and uncle in the town where they had been martyred forty-eight years earlier for their testimony of Jesus Christ.

While in Karadesh, Dad insisted on taking a swim in the sea. He had always told me that the beach there was the best in the world. When he was young, people swam at night under the moonlight instead of during the day.

That day we went to a nearby café to have a fish dinner. Our waitress could tell we were strangers. Dad struck up a conversation with her in Turkish, and for a while I thought they were not going to quit talking. I finally interrupted and said, "Tell us what you two are saying." When the waitress went to get our food, Dad turned to me and told me this story.

"This lady used to go to the Sunday school where your grandpa was the minister," he said. "She was thirteen years old when the Kurdish terrorists came and killed the men, the married women, and the male children. Since she was a virgin, one of the terrorists took her for his son's wife."

Our waitress had been an eyewitness to the massacre. She recounted for my father what had happened that day, how Kurdish terrorists seized my grandfather and gave him the choice to deny Christ or face death. She described how they had unceremoniously decapitated him when he declared his devotion to Christ. It was the story that had fueled my dislike of Kurds when I was young. All my life I had heard my relatives repeat the same angry phrase: "The Kurds killed your grandpa!" When we lived in Lebanon, I did not trust the Kurds there. But God wanted to heal that fracture in my soul, and he had brought me into contact many years later with a Kurdish leader so I would learn a life-giving lesson.

Whenever I thought about the Kurdish leader, I prayed for him and felt my soul released bit by bit from the bonds of enmity. For two years, Chris was unable to secure a license for his uplink. Then in September 1999, Chris e-mailed me:

"I have good news," he wrote. "I finally succeeded in finding an uplink. The Kurdish channel is on the air."

"One other thing, Elias," he concluded. "Would you come and visit me in Gibraltar, where my family and I live?"

I accepted his invitation, and, as we visited, I received more than I had bargained for.

GETTING THEM SAVED AND LEADING THEM TO CHRIST IS THE REVENGE, BECAUSE THE REAL ENEMY IS SATAN HIMSELF, AND HE HAS DECEIVED THOSE PEOPLE THROUGH THE CENTURIES.

"The Kurdish leader has given me two hours of airtime on his channel every morning to air whatever programs I wish," Chris said. "I have some good news for you: I want to put the *Good News* program on daily, three hundred and sixty-five days a year, for free."

I was flabbergasted.

"That kind of airtime costs half a million dollars, not to mention the other substantial costs," I said.

"I know," he said, smiling.

I couldn't help but think of Revelation 6:10–11, which says:

> How long, O Lord, holy and true, dost thou not judge
> and avenge our blood on them that dwell on the earth?
> And white robes were given unto every one of them;

and it was said unto them, that they should rest yet for
a little season, until their fellowservants also and their
brethren, that should be killed as they were, should be
fulfilled.

Now, after years of viewing Kurds in a negative light, God
made a way for me to preach the gospel over a Muslim Kurdish channel—for free. The Holy Spirit spoke to me and said,
"The revenge is to love your enemy. Be good to them that
hate you. Take the gospel to the children and grandchildren
of those that killed your grandfather. Getting them saved
and leading them to Christ is the revenge, because the real
enemy is Satan himself, and he has deceived those people
through the centuries."

The joy of the Lord overwhelmed me, and I began to
weep. I could hardly believe that God would give me the
privilege of preaching the gospel on the Kurdish Muslim
channel. I left Gibraltar. On the airplane I prayed, "O Lord,
my birthday is October 1. Let Chris tell me that the program will begin airing on my birthday." I got an e-mail
from Chris a few days later telling me that my program
would begin airing on October 1. And it did. I opened each
program, as always, in the name of Jesus, Son of the living
God; the One who died, was buried, and rose again.

Letters poured into our office in Cyprus in greater vol-
ume than ever, because now the program was on daily, not
weekly. Kurds from Kurdistan and Europe watched the program. People wrote saying they had dreams of Jesus talking
to them. Others told us that when I prayed, Jesus healed
them.

A forty-year-old Kurdish man living in Holland wrote to
tell me he had been a Kurdish Yazid, or devil worshiper,

which is a sect within Kurdish culture. But he suffered from a painful stomach condition. He prayed with me while watching the program, and his stomach was healed. He and his wife renounced Satan worship, were converted, and baptized in water. We sent him a Bible, and our office helped him grow in his newfound faith in Jesus Christ. I later met this man and his wife in person, and we aired an interview with them on our television program.

THE LIFE PATH I CHOSE, PIONEERED BY MY FOREBEARS, HAS PROVEN THE FAITHFULNESS OF GOD AT EVERY TURN.

With each testimony that came in from Kurdish viewers, I felt God was avenging the blood of the martyrs—the blood my forebears had spilled for the sake of the gospel. I had not pursued ministry to Kurds specifically, but God had brought me full circle to minister to the sons and daughters of those who had taken the lives of my grandfather and uncle.

God also brought me full circle to the original television station I had broadcast from in Israel. It was now on satellite and cable television in the Holy Land. I contacted the sales manager and purchased a slot of airtime, and since September 2002 the *Good News* program has once again been reaching the people who watched us in the early days of our TV ministry.

The life path I chose, pioneered by my forebears, has proven the faithfulness of God at every turn. He has protected my life, guided me when I did not know the way, and opened the door to take the gospel to the Middle East. For half a century I have ministered through that open door, believing that the only way to reach people is through the power and demonstration of the Holy Spirit accompanied by the love of God.

Today there are twenty-four-hour digital satellite channels reaching out to the Arab world. Some carry nothing but Arabic programming. The *Good News* program now airs in one hundred seventy-eight nations daily in the Arabic language.

That is my story. By God's grace, it is far from finished.

^ᴇ^ Epilogue ᴇ^

CHALLENGED TO LOVE:
SEPTEMBER 11, 2001

I N Sᴇᴘᴛᴇᴍʙᴇʀ 2001 I took a team of Americans with me to Cyprus for our leadership conference. Pastor Jim Tolle, senior pastor of The Church On The Way in Van Nuys, California, was with me, as was my son Tim. We had a memorable conference, but on September 11, in the middle of the conference, I happened to turn on the television. I saw the twin towers of the World Trade Center fall to the ground, and the images left me speechless. Many people began to panic and wanted to go back home immediately.

I was scheduled to preach in a large church in Portland, Oregon, on the sixteenth, but we heard that flights were being canceled. My son Tim decided to leave on the twelfth. I warned him not to, knowing he might get stuck in some airport along the way, but he wanted to go. Others left as well, but Jim and I stayed and took our flight from Cyprus to London two days later. I had never seen an airport so empty as Heathrow that day. We had to overnight in London, and when we returned to the airport the next morning, it was crawling with stranded people. Our airline had canceled its Los Angeles flight. The lines were long, and everybody wanted to get on the only flight going to the United States that day, which was going to San Francisco. Only those who were already booked, military personnel, and doctors were allowed to go. Though Jim and I were not booked, they took our tickets, and we waited to see if we would be fortunate enough to get on the plane.

As we were grabbing a bite to eat in an airport restaurant, I heard my name being called over the speaker. I rushed to the ticket counter, and Jim followed.

"Here is your seat, Dr. Malki," they said.

"What about my assistant?" I asked.

"We are only taking doctors and military personnel," they said. The only reason they had chosen me was because I had a "Dr." on my ticket—something I rarely did. I said good-bye to Jim and boarded. He remained in London for three days before they put him on a flight to Los Angeles. I was able to make it to the church in Oregon, and the pastor couldn't believe I had kept my commitment. We had a terrific service that Sunday morning.

The world changed after September 11, 2001, and my ministry had to change with it. The government of Cyprus would no longer allow us to bring Arab students into the country for three months at a time. Instead of shutting the facility down, we began hosting leadership conferences such as the ones we had held years earlier in Lebanon and Egypt. Pastors and church leaders from Jordan, Egypt, Israel, Syria, and Lebanon came, and the Lord blessed the conferences by refreshing those church leaders and baptizing many of them with the Holy Spirit. The attendees from Syria were especially needy because there is not a single full gospel church in Syria that is recognized by the government. The other evangelical churches there and in Lebanon are part of an evangelical organization that doesn't allow Pentecostals to be part of its membership. The governments of Syria and Lebanon will not recognize any evangelical ministry unless they come under the covering of this group. Leaders from Syria and Lebanon who arrived at our conferences with slumped shoulders and weary faces left looking lighter and full of joy because they received the fullness of the Holy Spirit. We held the conferences every three months.

I BEGAN TO SHARE WITH OTHER
BELIEVERS IN A SENSITIVE WAY THAT
CHRISTIANS ARE TO BE SALT AND LIGHT
TO ALL OF THE WORLD, NOT JUST TO
ONE GROUP OR ANOTHER.

After September 11, 2001, I was also disturbed to hear the change in the way Christians spoke of Arabs and Arab governments. Many Christians chose sides politically, supporting one government against others. They let their patriotism or national pride get in the way of their clear spiritual sense, and they effectively closed a door of opportunity for sharing the gospel in much of the Middle East.

Nowhere in the New Testament do I see Christians encouraged to support one government over another. The opposite was true: we are admonished to obey the laws of the country in which we reside and to pray for peace. *Yes*, I thought, *we should vote and have opinions.* But when pastors and leaders went on television and took sides in the conflict in the Middle East, they did great harm. They should have reminded people instead that Jesus said, "My kingdom is not of this world" (John 18:36).

> YOU CANNOT DESTROY AN IDEA WITH
> BOMBS. YOU MIGHT KILL ONE LEADER,
> BUT TWO MORE WILL RISE UP IN HIS
> PLACE. BUT THE CONFLICT CAN BE WON
> BY FOCUSING ON THE INNER MAN.

I began to share with other believers in a sensitive way that Christians are to be salt and light to all of the world, not just to one group or another. Governments will do their job, but we as the church should remain free and disentangled so we may preach the gospel to everyone—even those we consider political or national enemies. The minute we allow ourselves to be identified with one group or another, one nation or another, one race or another, we have lost our effectiveness as ministers of the gospel. Those who are offended cannot trust us any more and will not believe our message. As the Bible says, "A brother offended is harder to be won than a strong city" (Prov. 18:19).

I reminded my Christian brothers and sisters that the situation in the Middle East and the present world crisis would not get better. On the contrary, it would get worse. But to take sides against one nation or another was a trick of the devil to make us ineffective in reaching the very people who hungered for the true power of the gospel.

On the other hand, I was grateful that the conflict between the Western world and Al Qaida had focused the Western church's attention on the Arab world. Historically, before Arabs were exposed to Judaism, Christianity, and Islam, they were heathens like any other people. They had many gods, but did not know the true God. Islam came to the Middle East six hundred years after Christianity and literally took over many countries, militarily speaking. Most people in those countries converted to Islam, and the Arabic language became the language of the Middle East.

But the gospel had thrived in the shadow of Islam. The Bible was first translated into Arabic in my home city of Beirut by Presbyterian missionaries in the 1800s. Lebanon was then under Turkish rule. The Presbyterian missionaries were so dedicated to humanitarian service that in the 1800s, the largest American university outside the United States was in Beirut, Lebanon, as was the largest American hospital outside the States, both founded by Presbyterian missionaries from the United States.

This kind of ministry paid off among Catholics and Greek Orthodox who learned what it meant to be born again. My great-grandfather was among them. But to my knowledge, the full gospel message was not known until the break of the twentieth century when Assemblies of God missionaries went into the Middle East. They won early results and established indigenous churches in some countries, but the message was not effective among Sunni, Shiite, and Alawite Arabs, and it seemed the church gave up on these people until the advent of radio and television in the 1950s. The *Lutheran Hour* broadcast made some inroads but didn't bring many results. Then in 1977 the *Good News* program began airing on radio, and, in 1982, on television. For twelve years I was the only man on television presenting the full gospel in the Arabic language.

As the conflict against terrorism now overshadows the Western view of the Middle East, let us be reminded that the roots of terrorism cannot be destroyed with political or military power, because the roots of terrorism run deep into an idea and religious philosophy. But the gospel of Jesus Christ preached without compromise, with anointing and power, can change hearts that now are devoted to that idea. You cannot destroy an idea with bombs. You might kill one leader, but two more will rise up in his place. But the conflict can be won by focusing on the inner man. We do well to remember that "God so loved the world..." (John 3:16). By this, He meant every terrorist and every member of every religion in the world. We must have faith in the gospel, and, as the great apostle Paul said, stand up and say:

> I am not ashamed of the gospel of Christ: for it is the power of God unto salvation to everyone that believeth; to the Jew first, and also to the Greek.
>
> —Romans 1:16

How can we reach the Middle East for Jesus? By relying upon the Word of God alone as our weapon. The Word was the only weapon the apostle Paul had. Today we have a great opportunity to carry the Word worldwide by satellite television. This allows people to hear the Word of God in the privacy of their own living rooms, and the Bible tells us that faith comes by hearing, and hearing by the Word of God. Satellite television is a powerful tool to fulfill the words of Jesus that this gospel of the kingdom must be preached in all the world. As we bring the Word to the Middle East, it will be changed, and people who live in captivity to false ideas will discover liberty that comes from Jesus Christ who transforms them from the inside out.

Hitherto the Lord has helped us.
Our story *to be continued . . .*

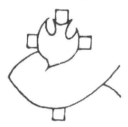

Middle East Gospel Outreach

Dr. Elias Malki

Dr. Elias Malki's television program, *Good News*, is aired on eight satellite television channels—one of which the program airs on four times a day. It is reaching 180 nations with an audience of 20 million people daily.

As an apostle, he has personally ministered in 20 nations of the world. He also ministers in churches of every size in America. He is a leadership conference speaker—specializing in evangelism, teaching on the Holy Spirit—and is an authority on the Middle East.

Dr. Malki is available to come and minister at your church or event. Please contact him at:

Middle East Gospel Outreach
P. O. Box 1891
Upland, CA 91785
Tel. (909) 981-0540
Fax (909) 981-4609
E-mail: em.mego@verizon.net

**Please see his Web site at
www.godsairforce.com for more information.**